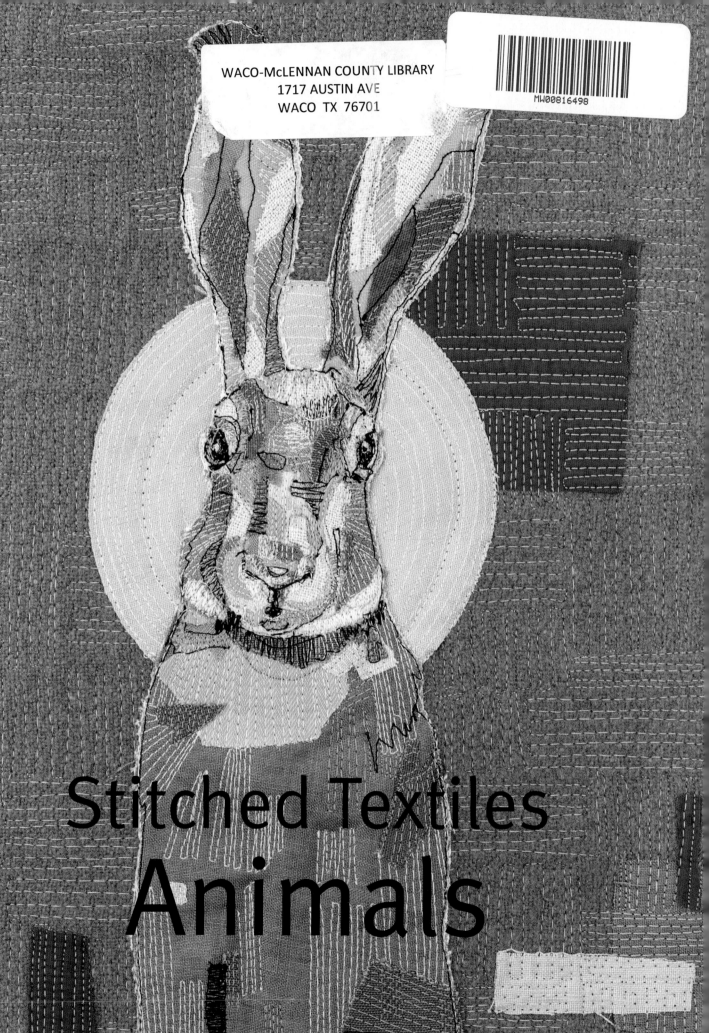

Stitched Textiles
Animals

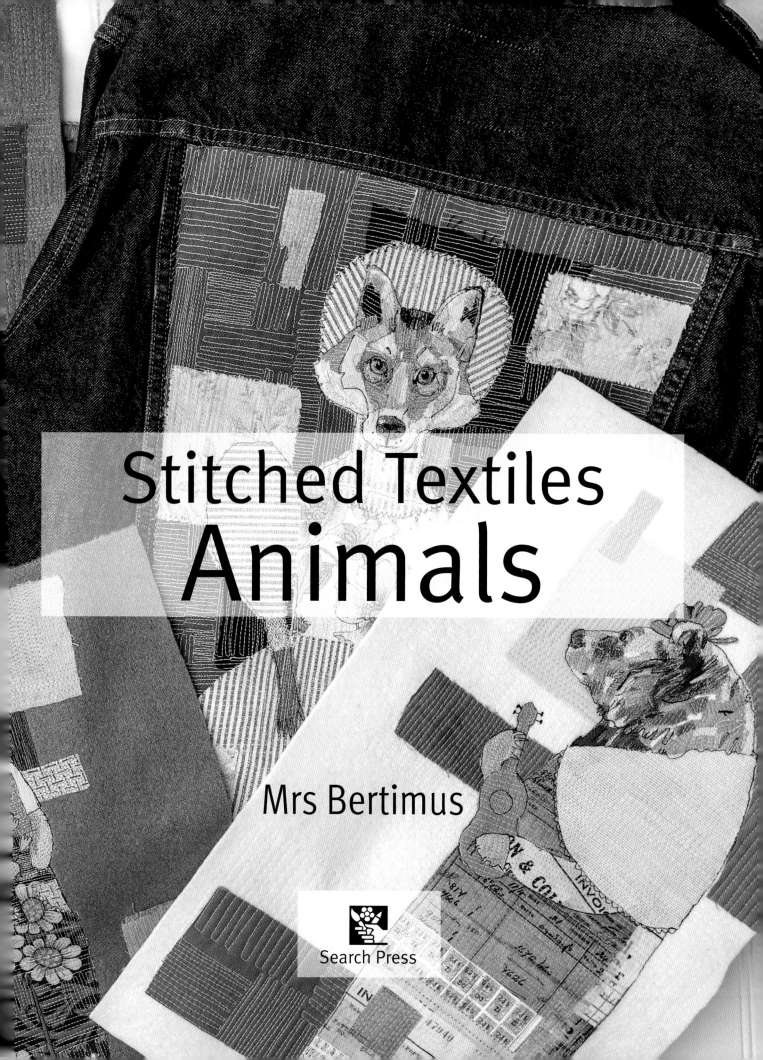

Stitched Textiles
Animals

Mrs Bertimus

Search Press

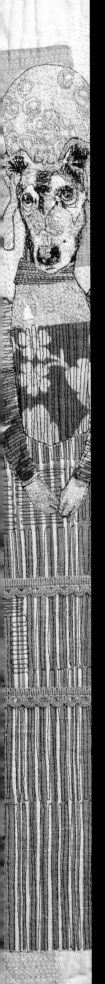

First published in Great Britain 2021

Search Press Limited
Wellwood, North Farm Road,
Tunbridge Wells, Kent TN2 3DR

Illustrations and text copyright
© Letitia Thompson 2021

Photographs by Mark Davison at
Search Press Studios

Photographs and design copyright
© Search Press Ltd. 2021

ISBN: 978-1-78221-822-7
ebook ISBN: 978-1-78126-789-9

The Publishers and author can accept no
responsibility for any consequences arising
from the information, advice or instructions
given in this publication.

Readers are permitted to reproduce any of
the artwork in this book for their personal use,
or for the purpose of selling for charity, free
of charge and without the prior permission
of the Publishers. Any use of the artwork for
commercial purposes is not permitted without
the prior permission of the Publishers.

Suppliers
If you have difficulty in obtaining any of the
materials or equipment mentioned in this book,
then please visit the Search Press website for
details of suppliers: www.searchpress.com

You are invited to visit the author's website at:
www.mrsbertimus.co.uk

Front cover
Midnight Fox
35 x 37.5cm (13¾ x 14¾in)

Page 1
Full Moon Hare
25.5 x 35cm (10 x 14in)

Pages 2–3
Ghost Hare
14 x 42.5cm (5½ x 16¾in)

Acknowledgements

Firstly I would like to thank Edward Ralph, my editor, for helping and
encouraging me every step of the way and for magically putting what
was in my head onto the page. I can never thank you enough for all
you have done for me.

Thank you so much Roz for finding me and for believing that
I could do this.

My thanks go to Mark for the fabulous photography and for making
me laugh during the portrait shots!

Thank you so much to Juan, Marrianne and Emma, for all the care and
attention to detail in the design of this book, and to all the rest of the
team at Search Press.

Thank you for everything, Ian, Lottie and Middie: I couldn't have done
this without you.

Huge thanks and love to my Mum and Tommy: you have always
supported my artistic adventures and dreams.

Thank you Nanna Dorothy and Auntie Maxine for sharing your stories.

My thanks go to Jean, Queen of the village, for telling me about
Mr Bertimus.

To Sam Christer and Debs Theobald, thank you both for your
friendship, help and laughs.

Many thanks go to the JLC Creative Arts Department; Kelly Boyd, Pat,
Julie and Laura Charley Robinson, for all the help, encouragement and
advice you have given me.

Thank you to my two very patient friends, Ginny and Hannah, for
helping me with Photoshop.

Thanks to the team at d4daisy, for their support and encouragement,
which gave me the confidence to pursue this book.

I'd also like to thank the amazing online community of artists,
creators and friends for your support and for keeping me company
as I work in my studio. For finding and supplying beautiful vintage
fabrics, trimmings, collage papers and inspirational ephemera, my
thanks go to:

Louise Presley: www.louisepresleyartist.com

Deborah Greensill: instagram.com/dsg1964

Wendy Shaw: instagram.com/ticking_stripes

Many thanks to Julie Steel and Emma Roberts of The Steel Rooms
(www.thesteelrooms.com) for your encouragement and friendship.

Thank you Louise Presley, for showing me that there was a place
for my textile art.

My heartfelt thanks to Louise Asher, for your constant support and
for inviting me to teach freestyle machine embroidery at the magical
Hope & Elvis Studio (www.hopeandelvis.com).

I'd also like to thank the wonderful community of creative souls whom
I have taught, both at my workshops and at college. You are all
an inspiration.

Contents

Introduction

For as long as I can remember I have been torn between fine art and textiles, and it took me a long time to realize that I didn't have to 'pick a team'. In fact, most of the principles that apply to painting also apply to machine embroidery; I find that each discipline supports the other.

Once I realized that all you needed was an embroidery foot, my sewing machine became a drawing machine. I am such a flibbertigibbet that I will happily flit from one to the other, and often the characters that appear in my paintings will pop up in my embroideries and vice versa.

Drawing, painting and stitching animals has always fascinated me. I really enjoy trying to work out the anatomy and describing the texture of fur. I produce representational animal artwork as well as more stylized, anthropomorphic characters. Animal faces are so expressive, and it is usually as I'm creating the embroidery or painting that a story or character begins to emerge. It's often the combination of a particular scrap of fabric and a quick snap of an animal – perhaps simply a dog that I've seen in the street, or a hare in a field – that sparks off an idea.

I don't approach my textiles practice as an embroiderer, but as a fine artist using the fabric as paint and the sewing machine needle as the pencil. Although I haven't been formally trained in the traditions of embroidery, it is such an expressive and adaptable genre. I just hope that I don't offend any embroidery purists!

As a teenager, my sewing machine offered me a chance to really express myself. As I could rarely buy new outfits before going on a night out (living in a small Northern town, I usually couldn't find the clothes that I wanted), every Saturday morning I would visit my local charity shop. There, I would chat to the lovely lady who worked there, and buy vintage 'granny dresses' that I would take home and use to whizz up an outfit before hitting the town. Years later, when I discovered machine-embroidery, my sewing machine offered me another way for self-expression and helped me to stitch my characters and stories.

I think that it is this innate sense of mending, fixing and patching that entwines embroidery with a sense of family and personal narrative. Whenever I am handling vintage fabrics and quilt pieces I feel a great sense of responsibility to 'do it justice' – but I also feel as though I am adding to its life story. When we take the time to repair or re-purpose a faded piece of textiles it becomes reflective of our own values – we shouldn't abandon those things of worth simply because they have become old or worn.

> *Once I realized that all you needed was an embroidery foot, my sewing machine became a drawing machine.*

Minuet

26 x 29cm (10¼ x 11½in)

Combining stories and characters with materials that have their own tales to tell is so rewarding; providing, as it does, an escape from the everyday world.

Sticky notes

You will see sticky notes with hints and tips written on them scattered throughout this book. I don't think that I could manage without my beloved sticky notes – they are an essential part of my creative process! In fact, most mornings when I wake up and pull back the duvet, a cloud of fluttering paper fills the air – if inspiration strikes in the middle of the night, I have to jot down the idea quickly!

Materials

Machine embroidery is a very forgiving technique. More often than not, a 'mistake' can be quickly patched over – and often leads to a more exciting result! You don't need mountains of material, either – the following pages explain what you'll need for the projects and techniques in the book, but you should absolutely feel free to experiment and play.

Fabrics

In my opinion you can't beat the texture, colour – and mysterious past life – of vintage and recycled fabric. Who knows what conversations that tattered lace tablecloth witnessed or the holiday romance that faded summer dress twirled through? As you can tell, I get rather carried away by pre-loved treasures – not only is the fabric often wonderful to work with, but the imagined history sparks many ideas and stories as I stitch on them.

Another advantage of working with such materials is that you will need to pop into second-hand shops to top up your supply of fabric – and that means you will always have the perfect excuse to dive into the delights of an unexplored charity shop or other treasure trove.

When cutting up clothing for your embroidery you can utilize some of the details, such as buttonholes or areas of decorative stitching, to enhance your design. Look out for rust marks and repairs when selecting vintage or antique fabrics, as these add a real sense of history and character to your work.

Open-weave materials and lace are useful for adding surface texture – oh, how I love 1960s' linen tea towels and bark cloth! – and I often incorporate patterned fabrics into the costumes of my animal artworks.

Linen This is such a lovely fabric to work on, especially when it has been washed and used over the years as the texture softens and the colour fades. Most of the linen that I use has been recycled from second-hand clothing or tablecloths.

Cotton Different weights of cotton fabric provide a wide variety of textures and surfaces to work on. A heavyweight cotton drill can be useful for background blocks of colour, while lightweight scraps of cotton can be used to add subtle tonal variations and detail on areas such as faces.

Bark cloth Whenever I spot an old 1960s' curtain at a car boot sale, my heart skips a beat – I absolutely love stitching onto bark cloth. The thread seems to 'sink' into the deliciously soft material and it creates a beautiful surface texture. Bark cloth is often printed with the most amazing (and sometimes quite crazy) patterns. Applying areas of pattern into your embroidery can really add a 'pop' of energy into your design. I often incorporate small snippets of bark cloth in my work as there is usually a wide range of colours and tonal variations to use because of the printed pattern.

Lace Open-weave materials and lace are useful for adding surface texture and for adding tiny details to the animals' costumes. I also find scraps of lace useful for 'knocking back' areas of shadow, as it softens the edges of the darker-toned fabric (see *Midnight Fox* on page 108 for an example).

Woollen blanket Vintage woollen blankets are always on my charity shopping wish list. They create a beautifully soft but stable backing for stitched pieces. Blanket-stitched or fringed edging can also add an attractive decorative feature.

Clean your machine

Do try to clean out your sewing machine's bobbin case regularly after stitching through blanket, as fluff can build up very quickly. (I am such a hypocrite, as I am the worst for putting off such tasks; but it does make a difference to your machine's performance!)

A selection of fabrics from my ever-growing and changing collection.

Embroidery materials

The most important tool here is a sewing machine, but the other bits and bobs listed will give you more options. It's worth noting that you don't need a really complicated sewing machine: instead, enjoy using your own sewing machine and getting to know its quirks and idiosyncrasies – when you really understand your machine, it will become like an extension of your hands.

In fact, I've only ever owned two sewing machines. When I bought my trusty Brother sewing machine (see below) a few years ago, I had to have a little chat to my original New Home machine that I got for Christmas when I was thirteen!

Sewing machine My machine is a Brother Innov-is 55, but any machine that allows you to lower the feed-dogs (what a lovely phrase) is suitable for machine embroidery.

Machine embroidery foot You will need to replace the presser foot that comes as standard with most machines with an embroidery foot. These are not expensive, but check that it is suitable for the model of sewing machine that you own.

Sewing thread I find Gütermann sew-all – a polyester sewing thread – is perfect for machine embroidery as it is so durable. It comes in such a wide range of colours. I also like to use Gütermann's top stitch thread for hand stitching because it is slightly thicker than normal sewing thread.

Embroidery thread I have collected a variety of hand-embroidery threads which are useful for final hand-stitched embellishments. I favour Gütermann Sulky Rayon 40, as this thread has a beautiful sheen and I use this occasionally when adding a final layer of machine stitch. I find it especially useful when stitching fur.

Fusible web This is an adhesive web with a paper backing that can be ironed onto fabric. I find it really useful when I want to apply sharper, more graphic shapes to my designs. The double-sided adhesive makes it much easier to attach intricately shaped pieces onto the base fabric.

Tear-easy stabilizer This stabilizer is really handy when using a thick fabric or blanket as a backing, as it allows you to embroider your subject separately onto the stabilizer without any puckering or distortion. The stabilizer can be easily torn away without damaging the stitches, after which you can stitch the final layers onto the backing, instead of having to sew through all the layers of fabric.

Lutradur This is a bonded fabric and is available in a variety of weights. It begins to bubble and forms holes when heat is applied with a crafting heat tool. Lutradur can be coloured using paints or dyes and can be stitched and embellished.

Embroidery tissue paper I use this to trace the outline of my design for the final layer during the embroidery process. The thin paper is really easy to remove without damaging the stitches.

Tracing paper The thickness of tracing paper makes it perfect for transferring the embroidery design. I then draw around the cut-out pieces with an air-erasable pen.

Fabric glue Useful to secure fabric pieces before stitching, otherwise small pieces tend to lift up with the needle; and you may also catch the corners when you are machine embroidering. Always make sure that the glue is dry before you begin sewing, though, to avoid damaging your machine.

Air-erasable pen I use an air-erasable pen for drawing around template pieces onto the fabric. As the name suggests, the ink slowly disappears as it is exposed to air. The time it takes to fade away will depend on the type of fabric used. Other similar brands are available, but I find the purple ink of Madeira's Magic Pen makes it visible on both light and on dark fabrics. Always test out the pen on your fabric beforehand, though, just in case.

Iron A good iron is so useful throughout the whole process. You will need to press your fabric pieces and scraps so that it is easier to cut out and arrange them accurately.

Pressing cloth Sometimes called an ironing cloth, this will protect your fabrics from being scorched by the iron. You may want to have a second ironing cloth on hand, dedicated for use with materials such as fusible web. It will protect your iron from becoming damaged by the adhesive.

Textile foil I like to apply metallic textile foil to my work by backing it with fusible web and ironing it onto the fabric. The textile foils come in a variety of colours and patterns.

Fabric scissors You will need a good, sharp pair of scissors for cutting your fabric. Try not to use your fabric scissors for cutting paper, as the blades will become dull.

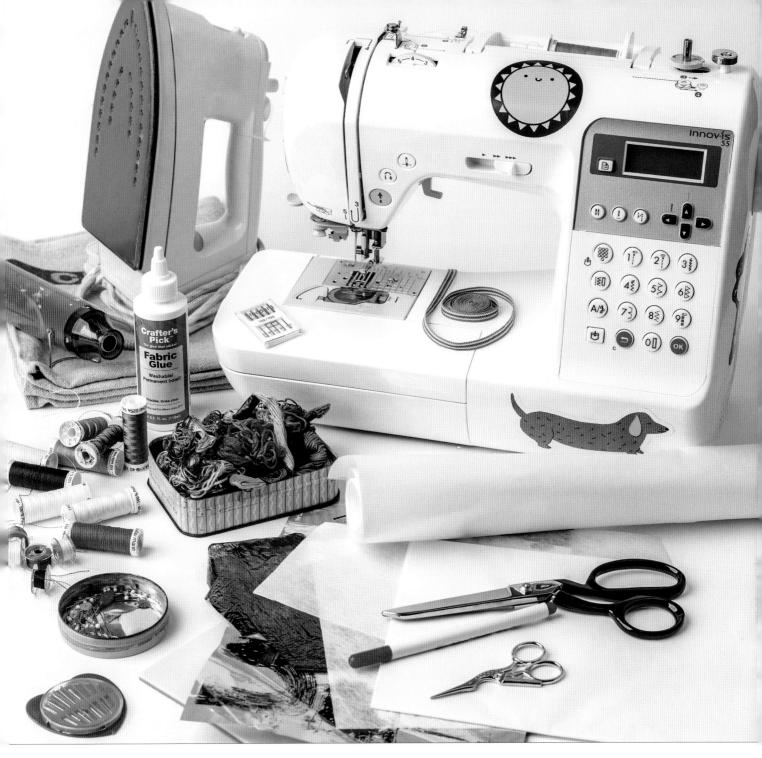

Embroidery scissors These small, sharp scissors are used throughout the embroidering process so that you can snip away any loose threads as you work. It can get very messy if you don't keep control of all those loose ends!

Crafting heat tool This is a handy tool for a wide variety of textile and art techniques.

Pins I find that glass-headed pins are useful because they are easy to spot if you drop them on the floor. They are also heat-resistant – you don't want to have melted plastic on your work after you've given it a good pressing!

Needles I use standard universal machine needles for all the techniques in this book. I also have sharps and crewel needles for hand embroidery.

Pictured here are my embroidery tools and materials. Don't feel restricted to the particular brands that I use; these are personal choices, and you should experiment to find those that suit you and your way of working best.

Art materials

You may find that you have many of these materials around the house already. Keep an eye out in DIY shops, car boot sales and supermarkets – you may well find something that creates an exciting new mark.

Pencils An HB pencil is perfect for tracing the templates, as you will need an accurate line. I favour Blackwing pencils for drawing as they produce a lovely rich variety of tones.

Olive oil I use this to help create a lovely smooth surface on which to draw.

Graphite stick A chunky graphite stick is such a lovely medium to draw with, it's great for expressive mark-making and using this makes it impossible to become too caught up in drawing tiny details!

Heavyweight cartridge paper You will need a good quality paper for the collaging techniques that are covered in the book.

Lining paper This paper has such a lovely surface to print on and you can buy a roll from the DIY shop very cheaply.

Office printer paper I find that this is the best type of paper to clean your gel plate on while you are printing. The bonus is that these papers can be fantastic for collaging too!

Acrylic paints I generally use Winsor & Newton, Daler-Rowney and Golden brands of acrylic paint. Acrylic paints are water-based, fast drying and versatile. I'll tell you about my favourite paint colours and mixes later in the book.

Gouache paint I love the matt finish of this water-based paint and I really enjoy using it when I'm drawing with a graphite stick.

Acrylic gel medium I use Golden's gel medium to apply and seal collage pieces.

Interference medium Daler-Rowney's interference medium creates a shimmering, iridescent effect over the top of paint. The medium is available in a variety of colours and it is perfect for projects like the *Cornish Herring* gel-plate print on pages 60–61.

Synthetic paintbrushes I generally prefer flat brushes but any type of artist paintbrush will be fine.

Gel printing plate This mono-printing plate from Gelli Arts is durable, easy to use and can produce a wide variety of effects that can be layered. The plate can be used to print on many different types of surfaces including fabric and paper. I use acrylic paints when printing.

Catalyst silicone wedge tools These mark-making tools are made from flexible silicone and you can create a varied range of patterns, from the bold to the delicate. It is a perfect tool to use with the gel printing plate because it won't scratch or damage the printing plate surface.

Glue stick Power Pritt is my favourite type of glue for collage. It's convenient, bonds paper and card really well and doesn't create bubbles under the paper's surface.

Rags A cut-up t-shirt is the best type of rag to use for wiping out shapes on the gel plate.

Craft knife and blades These are so useful when cutting out precise and delicate pieces of paper for collaging. I use a Swann Morton blade set – a no. 3 handle and 10A blades. Whatever brand you choose, please use them carefully in conjunction with a self-healing cutting mat.

Sticky notes I cannot express how much I adore sticky notes! They are so useful for masking areas when you are gel-plate printing and can be used to create sharp edges when printing and drawing.

Masking tape This tape is perfect for fixing the edges of fabric or paper to your work surface when gel-plate printing. It can also be used to create sharp edges when gel-plate printing on fabric, although I would use sticky notes for this purpose if I were printing on paper.

Masking film If you need to mask off shapes that are more complex than simple squares or rectangles, this film can be cut into whatever shape you need. You can also trace your design onto the film before cutting out which is very handy indeed. I use Frisket's matt low-tack version.

Found objects Finding materials to use for printing is completely addictive! Try and experiment, just ensure that the materials you use won't scratch your gel plate. As a starting point, try sequin waste, or sticky foam shapes.

Extra-strength double-sided tape I use this to attach the textured materials onto a scrap piece of mount board to make printing plates.

Sketchbooks Anything you can draw in to capture your imagination will work. I am a fan of Moleskine sketchbooks because I love the smooth texture of the paper – it is perfect for mixed media.

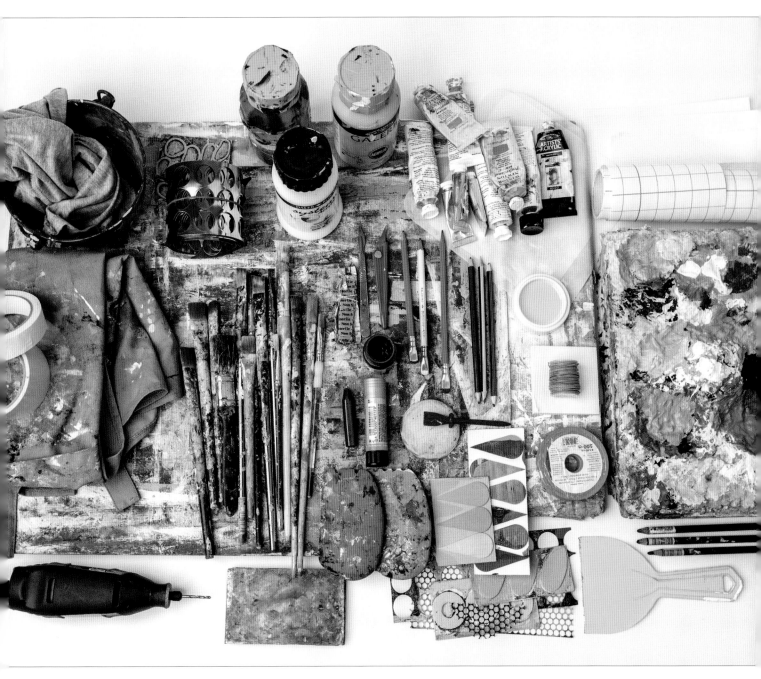

Hobby drill This is a really versatile power tool and I've had great fun experimenting with this when distressing fabric surfaces. Always follow the instructions carefully – I still feel a bit scared when I use my Dremel 3000 drill! – I use a clamp (not pictured) and a scrap piece of wood to drill into to protect the work surface.

Water pot Any container can be used as your water pot, my favourite is an old billy can that I picked up at a car boot sale.

Palette I use a stay-wet palette, which keeps my acrylic paint workable for longer. An old plate or recycled plastic lid is perfectly fine if you are not using a large amount of paint.

Apron I would advise that you wear an apron or old shirt to protect your clothes if you are printing or painting.

Building your own collection of art materials over time creates an individual and highly personal set of expressive possibilities.

13

Where to start

This section of the book leads you through the creative process, teaching you all of the basic techniques, from finding your inspiration to the practical aspects of adapting the image in your mind into a textile art design, and then to completing the piece with stitch.

Inspiration

You can refer to a photograph, drawing or other primary source as a starting point; but inspiration can be taken from everywhere. Sketching from life, photographing something that catches my eye, visiting museums and galleries, childhood memories, reading folk tales and listening to music are just some of the sources of inspiration that I refer to time and time again.

Whenever an idea pops into my head (be it for a certain colour palette, subject matter or technique combination), I will always try to jot it down or write it in the notes section of my phone.

I also keep a journal where I might try out technique experiments, write down more personal notes and stick in tiny scraps of left-over ephemera. I often flick through this when I'm stuck and I frequently find that it can kick-start a new piece of work – I'll show you an example later, when we look at *The Mad Hatter's Mouse* on page 86.

Engaging with your subject

I think it is really important to try to draw as much as possible. If you feel unconfident about this, remember that no one has to see it! Try to draw from real life as much as you can, as well as from your imagination or photographs. My sketchbooks are messy, full of scribbles and notes, but they capture the moment more effectively than any photograph could.

Sometimes it's impossible to work from a primary source, in which case secondary sources of inspiration, such as magazine images or pictures from the Internet, are useful. This is for two main reasons:

• Most wild creatures are very elusive.

• I haven't got a pet hare or fox!

When referring to secondary sources, it can help to look at more than one photograph when you are designing your embroidery so that you avoid slavishly copying it.

Sketching from life
I sketched and photographed this greyhound while sitting in a café. I love the shape of these beautiful dogs and their faces are so full of character. Working from life allows you to sketch quickly, enabling you to record the most important essence of whatever captured your attention. Animals don't stay still for very long!

Putting yourself in your work

My nanna often talks about how she used to embroider flowers on her father's flannel shirts and how she would draw around a cotton bobbin along the edge of the bedsheets and then blanket stitch around them. The concepts of cherishing your possessions and of adding decoration and beauty to everyday belongings has been woven into my upbringing. My mum would make all my clothes (my parents were hippies and she would make me my own tiny flared trousers) and there was always painting, baking or stitching going on. Your artwork is personal, so look close to home for inspiration.

Choosing colours: my palette

My thoughts here explain the choices I make for colour, but the sky is the limit. Developing your own colour palette is a highly individual process, and even though I rarely use 'jewel-bright' or primary colours myself, please don't let me influence your personal sense of visual expression.

Fabric colours

A limited palette forms the basis for most of the creatures I stitch. Greys, neutrals and white are the staple colours of my fabrics because they act as the perfect foil for the limited colour palette that I enjoy using in both my painting and stitching. While I find sludgy blues, acid-sharp mustards and mucky pinks useful as accent and background colours, the 'backbone' for most of my embroideries is made up of the beautifully subtle spectrum of greys – from the lightest to the darkest tonal values and of the cool and warm varieties.

I also love adding black fabric to a design, especially if it needs to be more dramatic. It can also create a sharply defined edge if it is placed behind a part of the animal. I feel like a bit of a rebel when I use black because at some point in the past, I had been told that artists should not use black paint. It wasn't until many years later that I stopped feeling guilty about it when I painted. Now, Mars black is one of my favourite paints and I revel in its inky lusciousness. Remember, rules are made to be broken.

I have snipped from this particular grey linen dress during the last few years – I am starting to panic now as there is precious little left!

Jackdaw and Limpets
41.5 x 31cm (16¼ x 12¼in)

This piece beautifully demonstrates how useful black is for adding drama to a design: this colour really packs a punch. As mentioned opposite, black helps to define the sharp edges of a subject, such as the light-toned limpets in the top left-hand corner. You can see here that the reverse is also true, with the light background fabric and background blocks helping to bring out and define the black subject.

Paint colours

My favourite acrylic paints are titanium white and fluorescent red from Daler-Rowney's System 3 range; pale olive from Winsor & Newton's Galeria range; Mars black, potter's pink and yellow ochre from Winsor & Newton's Professional range; and teal from Golden. I use the muted, subtle colour combinations shown below because they work well with the neutral palette base that I use. These colours reflect the natural world and suit the animal subjects that I enjoy stitching.

Mixing tips

Use a different brush for each colour mix. This will help to keep your colours clean.

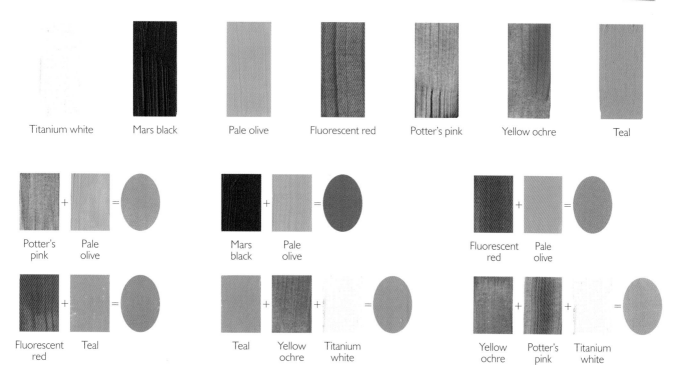

| Titanium white | Mars black | Pale olive | Fluorescent red | Potter's pink | Yellow ochre | Teal |

Potter's pink + Pale olive =

Mars black + Pale olive =

Fluorescent red + Pale olive =

Fluorescent red + Teal =

Teal + Yellow ochre + Titanium white =

Yellow ochre + Potter's pink + Titanium white =

Making your drawing

With your idea in mind, colours selected and reference to hand, you can start drawing out your design. When you are drawing, it is important to consider the underlying anatomical structure, and not simply focus on the fur or markings. This will help you to create designs that contain lots of surface interest, which will be useful when later translating the design into your fabric collage prior to stitching.

I know this sounds obvious, but really look at your subject before you begin drawing. It's tempting to rush into the actual drawing, but spending just a couple of minutes carefully observing can make all the difference.

At this early stage, try to find the abstract shapes on the animal's features (these are usually indicated by strong tonal values). It is really useful to draw these in when designing your embroidery, as it helps to suggest the three-dimensional form. In turn, this helps with the fabric selection process later on.

During the stitching process, this drawn anatomy will initially be depicted using a darker thread, even if it needs to be 'knocked back' later. The dark thread helps to define the main sections of your design.

The importance of tone

Recognizing the light, medium and dark tonal values of the subject matter is essential for a machine embroidery design because it will help you to focus on the three-dimensional form, without the added confusion of selecting the colour palette for the piece.

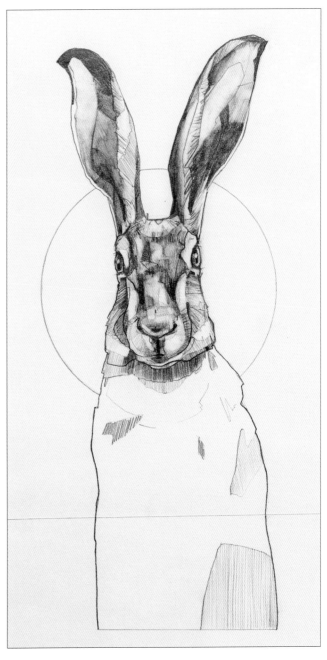

Pink Moon Hare plan

Carefully consider the subtle range of tonal values as you refine your design from the initial sketch, and begin to draw out the plan for your piece.

Initial sketch

This drawing shows the abstract shapes visible on this hare's head, which helps to identify the three-dimensional form. Considering the tonal values of the areas surrounding the subject itself can also be useful at this stage.

High contrast

One of my tutors at college once said to me when I was drawing that it helps to place the 'lightest lights next to the darkest darks' – this really helps to suggest the three dimensions of the anatomical structure.

Identifying tone

Drawing an object such as this sheep's skull is a really useful warm-up exercise that involves observational skills and helps you practise identifying light, medium and dark values without the added complication of colour. Before you begin, wipe a piece of kitchen towel dipped in olive oil over a sheet of good quality cartridge paper. This creates a beautiful surface to work on and the pencil seems to glide over the paper, creating a luxurious velvety quality of line.

For this exercise, I chose a sheep skull because of its interesting structure and surface texture, but you can refer to any reference material. Lightly rub a little more olive oil over the top of the areas you wish to blend, as this will soften and merge the darker tonal areas.

Materials

3B drawing pencil
Olive oil
Heavyweight cartridge paper

Keeping clean

When using this technique, add some extra sheets of paper in between your drawings or the oil will seep through the pages and possibly stain your artwork.

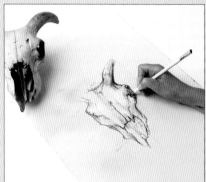

1 When you feel ready, place your pencil at the point you wish to start drawing the subject. Keep your eyes on the subject, not the paper, as you begin.

2 Move your eyes slowly around the subject, and move your pencil at the same speed your eyes are travelling, so that your eye and hand are working in a synchronized manner. Take it really slowly and carefully and be aware of the hand–eye co-ordination. It's almost like you're a drawing robot!

3 When all the tonal variations have been blocked in and blended with the oil, the final darker outlines can be added to any parts that need 'sharpening' up or redefining.

This drawing shows the anatomy and posture of the fox clearly; try identifying the major areas of tonal value that I have picked out in the fur.

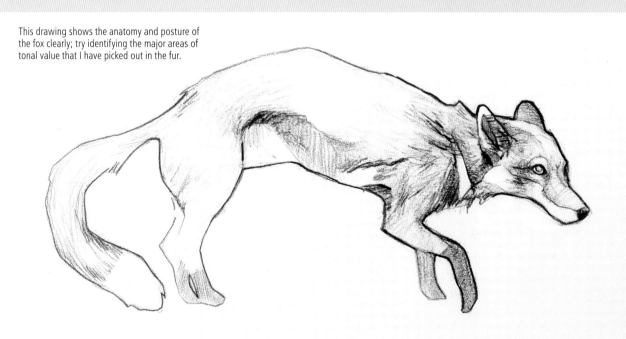

Tonal value maps

A tonal value map helps you to break down your drawing into simple abstract shapes that outline the main areas of tone – that is, the light, medium and dark areas. Drawn on tracing paper, you can then cut out the abstract shapes and use them as templates for cutting your fabric.

Taking the time to prepare a basic tonal value map from your drawing will help give you a sense of clarity, especially at the beginning of a project. Only the main tonal value blocks are mapped out, because the smaller shapes can be added during the stitching process itself – I usually add the final tiny highlights right at the end of the process.

Sketch only

The original sketch includes lots of subtlety of tone, as areas blend smoothly into one another. Since fabrics are flat colour, we can't easily simulate these gradients, and so need to break them up.

Sketch and overlay

With the tracing paper laid over the sketch, we can identify and outline the areas of tone. Some are obvious, while others will require you to decide whether to break up areas or not. The areas marked A and B are a good example of where I decided to establish breaks in a subtle area of tonal gradation.

Overlay only

Once the overlay is removed from the drawing, we are left with just a series of outlined abstract shapes that mark the main areas of tone. These are the shapes that will be cut out from your fabric.

Identifying values

Categorizing the tonal values in an organized, analytical way really helps you to design tonally, which I believe is much more effective than simply trying to replicate a subject's local colour.

I have tried to be quite specific when doing this and used the following simple labelling system to break tones down into six distinct groups, ranging from the lights to the darks:

LL Lightest-light

L Light

LM Light-medium

M Medium

MD Medium-dark

D Dark.

Making a visual map of these areas will help you to simplify your selection of fabrics because you are primarily basing your choice on their tonal value. It can be overwhelming when faced with a huge pile of materials; breaking it down to just six makes things more manageable.

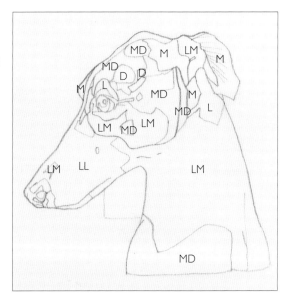

Overlay marked with values: the finished tonal value map

The values have been marked in here. We can now find six different fabrics, and match the areas one by one to the appropriate tonal value.

Making a tonal value map template

The skill here is making decisions on where to break up areas of similar tone. Try not to become too distracted by the smaller details until later on in the drawing and stitching process.

Materials

HB drawing pencil
Tracing paper

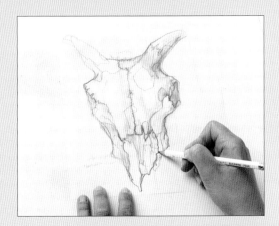

1 Place a sheet of tracing paper over your drawing. Use the pencil to trace the outline and the shapes of the different tonal value areas. Draw the main 'blocks' of the light and dark shapes first because the areas left will form the mid-tonal values.

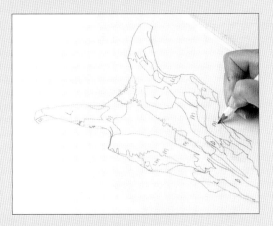

2 Lift the tracing away. Referring to the object and drawing, carefully label the values on the tracing as described to the right.

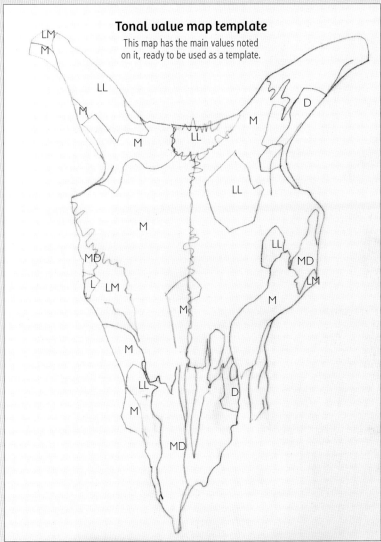

Tonal value map template
This map has the main values noted on it, ready to be used as a template.

Working from photographs or life

Rather than a drawing, you can use a photograph of your chosen subject matter to make your tonal value map. You can also use a three-dimensional object instead, in which case you need to draw it out first. Having a solid, three-dimensional object to refer to alongside the drawing as you are sewing is interesting and useful.

Fabric collage

Once you have prepared your tracing paper template, it's time to build up the design with fabric collage. Start by laying out your fabrics in tonal value piles that match the six values marked on your value map. It's a little bit like squeezing out your different paints on a palette before starting to paint.

Next, place the tracing paper template onto a mid-toned backing fabric. Using the template to guide you, cut out the whole shape (in this example, the whole deer's head) from fabric. This will be the base that all the smaller pieces of the design will be stuck onto using fabric glue.

Web or glue?

I use fusible web to attach large pieces to the fabric base, but for smaller pieces, it can be awkward to use. Use fabric glue for these instead.

Preparing the fabric pieces

Here, we use the tonal map by cutting out the pieces of the template one by one, then tracing around them on the corresponding piece of fabric in the relevant tonal value. Finally, we cut out the fabric shapes and glue them, one by one, onto the base fabric. After this, the piece is ready to be stitched.

1 Use scissors to carefully cut out one of the shapes from the tracing paper copy of the template.

2 Place the shape onto the appropriately-coloured fabric and use the air-erasable pen to draw round the piece.

3 Staying within the air-drying pen line, carefully cut out the shape from the fabric.

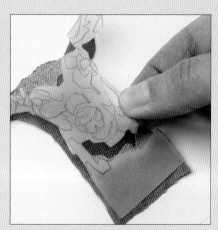

4 Lay the template over the embroidery to show you where the piece needs to sit – look for the hole you have just cut.

5 Use fabric glue to attach the piece to the embroidery, using the tracing paper to guide you.

6 Remove the template, then continue building up the picture in the same way to finish.

Using fusible web

Fusible web can be useful if the design is quite complex and has separate pieces that need to be assembled together. Here, as the deer's head, bodice and skirt pieces were cut out separately, using the fusible web as a backing helped to hold everything together before applying it to the background fabric. However, if the design isn't quite so intricate in its construction, simply using a small amount of fabric glue to attach your fabric pieces to the base is absolutely fine.

1 You need to assemble and secure the fabric collage before you begin. Here, I have glued the deer's head, bodice and skirt pieces together using a very small amount of fabric glue.

2 Place the assembled deer onto the rough side of the fusible web. Lightly draw around the deer's outline with a pencil.

3 Use scissors to cut out the fusible web, then carefully place the pressing cloth over the piece. Press with a warm iron for a few seconds.

4 Turn the piece over to check that the fabric has properly bonded. The image above shows the back of the deer with the fusible web bonded to it. The backing is still in place.

5 Being careful not to burn your fingers, peel off the backing.

6 Lay the deer onto the backing fabric, and using the iron and pressing cloth, bond the subject onto the backing fabric. Allow the fabric to cool completely before you begin stitching.

Freestyle machine embroidery

To set up your machine for freestyle machine embroidery, you will need to lower the feed dogs. Next, remove the standard presser foot and attach a free-motion embroidery foot. There are a variety of freestyle machine embroidery feet available: always check which embroidery foot is suitable for your machine. The particular foot that I use for embroidery is the Brother open-toe free motion quilting foot.

Next, set the stitch length. I tend to use 2.5mm, but experiment with your own machine to see which length works well for you. You can then thread the machine. To begin stitching this piece, I threaded both the top and bottom with a light cream thread.

Basics

Before you begin a section, make three or four stitches back-and-forth to secure the thread. Holding your hands in a triangle, as shown, will help you keep control. As you stitch, try to keep the fabric taut.

Back-and-forth stitch

Working straight lines back-and-forth helps to secure the fabric in a decorative way. It's meditative and reminiscent of ploughing.

Sketching stitch

Trailing the stitches in loops or waves is useful to describe shapes like the flowers of this floral crown.

Shaping stitch

This is great to suggest organic forms, like this ear – simply work in lines that follow the contours of the area.

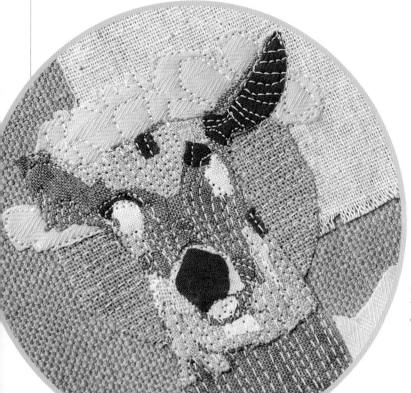

Feed dogs

If you can't drop the feed dogs on your sewing machine, you can instead cover them with a cover plate to make the machine ready to use for free machine embroidery.

Combining the stitches

The three basic stitches above can be combined in numerous ways, to produce an almost infinite variety to use on your textile artwork.

Outlining

Adding black outlines really pulls the design together and helps to define the key details of the embroidery.

1 Pin a tracing of the image outline, made on embroidery tissue paper, to your prepared fabric.

2 Thread your machine with black thread in both top and bottom bobbins; all settings are otherwise the same as for freestyle machine embroidery. Place the piece in and begin stitching round the outlines.

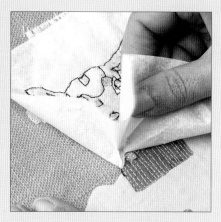

3 Once completed, remove the piece from the machine. Tear away the embroidery tissue paper. It is thinner than tracing paper, so won't damage the stitches.

5 This is what I call 'the ugly stage' because the lines can appear harsh and cartoon-like. You may need to 'soften up' the lines in some areas by stitching over in light or medium grey thread.

4 Pick away any remaining bits of embroidery tissue paper with a pointed tool.

Back of the work

I don't always snip the threads from the back as I work. This saves time and helps you to stay in the 'flow' as you stitch. Once you have finished stitching in one area, stitch back and forth three or four times to secure, raise the needle and gently pull the fabric away from the machine so that there is a short length of thread from the underside. Snip the top thread off and place the needle where you want to start stitching again. You will have to trim the bottom threads fairly regularly though, to avoid creating a huge tangle!

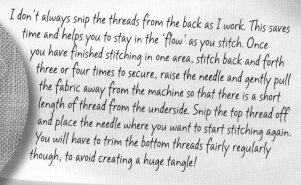

Softening the outlines

Now the lightest and darkest tonal values can be added by using the white and black thread for the final layers of stitching. This final layer really helps to sharpen up the embroidery. Areas such as the eye and nose can be defined and small details can be added to the costume and fur.

Be careful not to 'over-do it' at this stage, or the embroidery can become a bit too fussy and over-worked.

After the softening stage, the result is a lot more subtle and blended. This process also helps to unify the separate pieces of fabric in the embroidery.

A. Outlining the main shapes helps to create structure. The bold, fluid lines contrast with the more formal, ordered back-and-forth stitching in the background.

B. Back-and-forth stitch has been used to create a loose chequerboard design in the background, which also suggests a canvas-like texture.

C. Horiztonal stitching across the ochre circle helps to break up the predominantly vertical stitching on the body and neck.

D. Here, the sketching stitch helps to suggest the fullness of the sleeves and breaks up the flatness of the bodice area.

E. The back-and-forth stitch is used to create a very flat area that contrasts with the detailed face section. The stitch lines also help to knock back the busy floral pattern of the skirt.

Varvinter
20 x 28cm (8 x 11in)

Freestyle machine embroidery on vintage and recycled fabric, I named this deer 'Varvinter' because the Swedish word *vårvinter* is used to describe the time of year between winter and spring. I thought that this suited the fresh colour palette and floral costume perfectly: she seems to be quietly welcoming the first signs of spring.

Sheep skull

Another finished example, this shows how the sheep skull exercise from earlier can be worked up into a finished artwork. Why not have a go yourself?

As a base fabric, I glued the whole skull shape and larger fabric blocks onto an old seed sack, but a mid-weight cotton material would work just as well.

Once the design was securely stitched down I added the smaller pieces of fabric directly from observation. Directly cutting the fabric pieces in this way really helps to 'free up' your work and creates a sense of life and spontaneity.

From beginning to end – shown here is the initial inspiration – the skull itself (A) – the drawing (B), the tonal map on tracing paper (C), fabrics (D) and the final piece (E). The tonal map itself is normally destroyed in making the piece, so the example below is a replica.

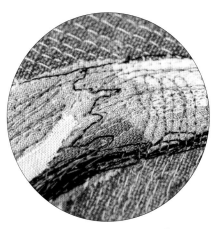

You can see some of the abstract-shaped fabric pieces here. I stitched the pieces down initially using cream thread, changing the stitch direction to help describe the different surface planes of the skull. The effect is subtle but really helps to suggest the three-dimensional form.

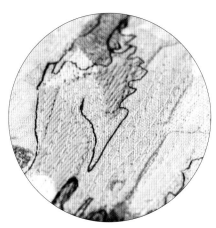

Black thread was used to bring the subject into focus once all the pieces were secure. Be careful not to stitch around every detail, otherwise your design can become very 'flat'.

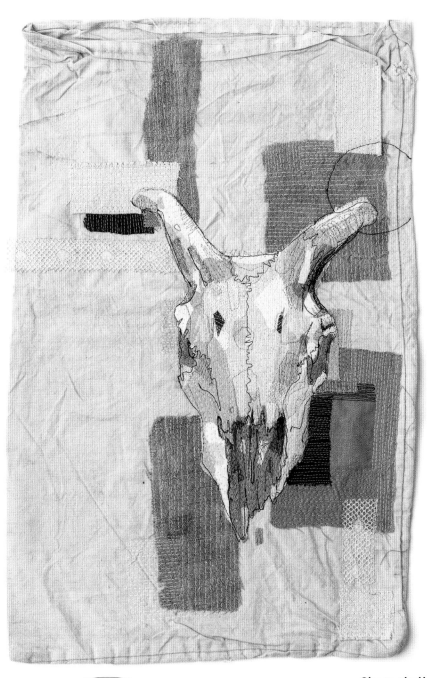

Sheep skull
29 x 44cm (11½ x 17¼in)

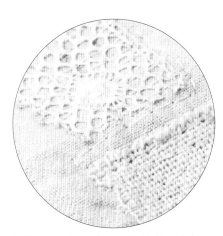

I added small pieces of lace as highlights and also to add interest and depth to the surface texture. The addition of strips of lace to the background helps to unify the composition as a whole.

This shot of the back of the base fabric shows the texture of the seed sack, which I thought really suited the subject matter.

Composition

I am the first to admit that I'm a huge geek when it comes to composing my designs, but don't let the theory tie you up in knots. It's there to help you when you need it, so don't let it dictate what you should or shouldn't do. Remember, creative souls love to break the rules.

This section of the book is here to help you if you feel as though something 'isn't quite right' with your design. These theories simply add to your tool kit of ways that may help you fix a creative problem. Always trust your gut first, and then if you're still not sure, apply the theory to see if it helps. There is no greater feeling than having a battle with your artwork and emerging victorious – you can do it!

On the following pages you will see how I develop the design for *Whitby Sheep*, from my initial photographs through to the finished piece on the next page.

Whitby Sheep
29 x 46.5cm (11½ x 18¼in)
The composition of this artwork is detailed on the following pages – read on to find out my creative process.

It's all about balance

There are no hard and fast rules about creating a visually pleasing, balanced composition, but there are some considerations that can help if you don't feel completely happy about the overall aesthetic of your composition.

- If you have placed a background shape on one side of your design, it can help to place another shape to counterbalance it on the other side.

- A bolder colour or darker tonal value placed in a muted, delicate setting, for example, would have a greater visual weight than one similar in colour or tone. The counterbalancing piece of fabric does not, therefore, necessarily have to be of an equal size.

- One of the most effective ways to create a sense of unity and cohesion in a composition is through the use of a limited colour palette.

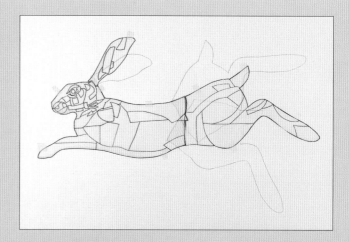

Staying flexible
This drawing shows both the initial design and some additional possibilities (in red and blue) for the hare on pages 69. Leaving some flexibility in the drawing allows you to be more adaptable as you create your composition. It also gives you the option of producing a series of other designs in the future.

Orientation – the horizontal and the vertical

One design guideline that is useful to keep in mind is that the horizontal and vertical line directions can suggest a subtle emotional quality, which can also help to strengthen the narrative element. The horizontal suggests a comforting, 'grounding' quality (if we see the horizon then we can navigate our way home)! The vertical suggests a more confrontational, challenging or hindering quality (think of a row of soldiers or a barricade that keeps you in or out).

These underlying perceptions are ingrained in our visual comprehension and we pick up on these messages subconsciously. You can allow one line direction to be dominant in a composition, or you may want to balance the opposing line directions to create a more harmonious design.

Composing *Whitby Sheep*

For this design I wanted to focus on the sheep without the inclusion of costume or props of any kind. The first things that really struck me were the strong shapes (both positive and negative) created by the horns and the abstract shapes within the sheep's fleece.

While these pages focus on a particular composition, they also give an overview of how I approach composition in general, a process which you can use yourself.

Collecting primary sources

I spent a lovely afternoon watching and photographing the sheep and their lambs enjoying the sunshine. After scribbling a few words and sketches down, I could feel the ideas starting to pop up in my head. After editing the photographs, I was eager to start drawing one of the sheep in particular. She had a very proud, almost regal character and looked me straight in the eye as I was clicking my camera.

I decided that I wanted the focus to be on the sheep's direct gaze. For this reason, I made the choice not to include the whole of the sheep's body or a potentially distracting background.

I took a number of shots of the sheep, some of which are shown above. I chose the image on the right as the main reference source for my design because of her direct gaze. The warm pinks and yellow ochres present on the sheep's horns, fleece and surrounding environment inspired the palette that I wanted to use.

Developing the sketch

The sketching process helps me to decide which areas need to be simplified. This is useful here because it allows me to ensure the focus is directed to the eyes and face.

Try to be as loose and free in your mark-making as possible when you start, as this helps to suggest movement. It is useful to lean your drawing hand on a scrap piece of paper when drawing in this way as it helps to minimize smudging your work across the paper.

At this stage, I also start to think about stitch direction possibilities and which parts of the design may need the definition of a black outline and which may not. I begin to 'block' in areas of the background and develop the more abstract shapes that could be found in the fleece.

It is important, however, not to stick too rigidly to your sketch. Use it as a loose guide rather than a strict plan. For example, cutting out abstract shapes while looking at your photographs or drawing can create really interesting shapes – and you will often find that the offcuts can also be perfect for your design.

Finalizing the drawing

When you start to feel more confident in the drawing, you can strengthen some of the marks that have been made to create a variety of line qualities. The quality of line can really pull certain parts of the drawing into focus and strengthen the sense of form and texture. Try to be selective when defining areas of the drawing: if you darken the whole of the outline, for example, your study will look flat and two-dimensional. This is really important when you are stitching in black thread at a later stage.

There are subtle ways to suggest form when defining outlines. In this example, I have drawn a darker line at the bottom of the chin, slightly inside the previous lighter outline. This little tweak can help to create a sense of depth.

I also used the side of the pencil lead and rolled it over the paper to create textured marks when drawing the wool. Drawing a frame around the sheep 'contains' the composition and it can help you to decide if the drawing could be developed into an embroidery design.

My drawing
I chose to use an old, slightly battered piece of cartridge paper for this drawing, as it provided a beautiful surface to draw on with a chunky graphite stick.

Identifying tones

With the drawing completed, the next stage was to use tracing paper to make a tonal value map template, as described on page 20.

The tonal value map shows that there is a large area of darker tones and visual interest in the facial area; this will help to direct the gaze to the intended focal point. However, because the sheep's body is predominantly a lighter tonal value, I will need to select a background fabric that is darker, otherwise the subject will become 'lost'.

Planning the stitches

The drawing stage definitely helped me in planning which type of stitches I would need for the embroidery. The shaping stitch would be essential for recreating the beautiful surface markings of the horns and the curved dome of the top of the skull. I also wanted to use the shaping stitch on the body to subtly suggest the movement of the wool. The sketching stitch would help to suggest the more 'scribbly' areas such as on the ear just next to the eye and under the sheep's chin.

The more uniform style of the back-and-forth stitch would help to calm down the background so that the composition wouldn't become too 'busy'.

Composition challenges

In building up the fabric collage, I identified some potential problems that I needed to resolve. The head section containing the most detailed visual information and the more dramatic range of tonal values creates two potential problems:

* The composition is cut in half horizontally with a busy top section and a quiet lower section. It's usually best to avoid splitting a composition in equal halves as it can appear quite obvious and not as visually interesting.

* At this stage of the process the head seems to be 'floating' because the body is almost invisible. Therefore, I decided to add an extra panel at the bottom in order to elongate the proportions of the design and avoid the 50:50 division of the composition design.

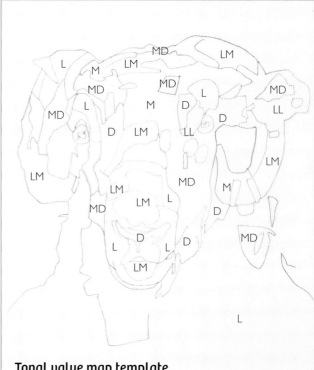

Tonal value map template

Starting the fabric collage
This early stage shows the fabric collage prior to addressing the challenges described to the left.

Refining the fabric collage

This page shows the finalized fabric collage, immediately prior to stitching. At this stage, the fabrics can still be moved about. Note how the sheep's body collage blends into the white background, despite the addition of contrasting elements of fabric. Compare this with the finished piece on page 31. The background fabric there is darker than the sheep's body so that it stands out.

A. In the finished piece, I added a block of fabric to the background at the top right (see detail, above) in order to balance the panel that I added to the bottom. Note that the colour of the negative space inside the right horn is different from that in the left, in order to create visual interest.

B. The strong curve of the sheep's horn is counterbalanced by the direction of the abstracted wool shapes. This creates a gentle visual flow through the whole design – as you can see by the arrows.

C. Because they are incorporated into the sheep's face and body (and background, in the finished piece), the small scraps of pink fabric help to unify the composition as a whole.

D. This piece of fabric acts as a unifying element that links the sheep's body and the panel which I added onto the bottom of the background, as shown in the detail below.

Letting the character emerge

When I started this embroidery I had intended to create another version of my *Party Lurcher* design (see page 43), but this time I wanted to stitch a side view profile of this character. However, my initial plan was just not working out. I had tried a party hat (see bottom left), a crown, and even perched a bird on his head, but he was not happy. In fact, he was beginning to look downright annoyed!

After many hours of struggling I realized that he just didn't want to be what I had planned! One thing that really amazes me is that no matter how carefully you may plan a piece of work, in the end you have to let your subject's personality come through. Whether painting or stitching you are never fully in control. At this point I resorted to the only strategy that was left... I put my work down and had a cup of tea – never underestimate the power of the cuppa.

At last, inspiration struck, this earnest, pensive chap would be just perfect for a Napoleonic style hat (and he did seem to be a rather dashing canine version of Poldark!). As soon as I placed the hat on his head, the whole composition design fell into place. What is ironic is that the name of the greyhound I had initially sketched and photographed was Captain!

If you are working on a similar project, it can be helpful to trace around the subject's head and draw different options before committing to your decision. Knowing that you can't spoil the hard work that you've done means that you can try out all sorts of crazy ideas. Not only can this be great fun, but you will find that it can often lead to the most successful result.

Captain
17 x 25cm (6¾ x 9¾in)

Backgrounds

You can use any shaped pieces of fabric when composing an artwork, but I often incorporate squares and rectangles in my work, particularly in the backgrounds. These geometric shapes usually form the building blocks or 'scaffolding' for the overall image, and contrast with the more curved and organic silhouettes of the animals.

A composition should be considered holistically, and not as separate 'subject' and 'background' elements, as each part of the design is affected by the other. Therefore it can really help to include a tiny piece (or pieces) of the fabric that has been used for the subject in the background.

Choosing a background colour

It's always worth taking the time to choose the colour of the backing fabric when you're planning your embroidery because it can really make or break the piece.

For the examples on this page I stitched a selection of differently coloured backgrounds for my *Full Moon Hare* embroidery to show how colour can affect the emotional quality of the composition.

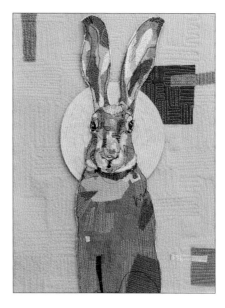

Warm background

This warm background colour integrates with the similarly-warm colour palette used in the hare itself. The overall quality seems quite soothing and restful.

Matching background

I used similar dark grey pieces of vintage cotton fabric for both the backing and the darkest tonal values on the hare itself. This has automatically created a unified palette and cohesive composition design. The cotton fabric was backed with a piece of woollen blanket so that it was sturdy enough to stitch on. I think that this dark background creates more of a dramatic, slightly mysterious effect.

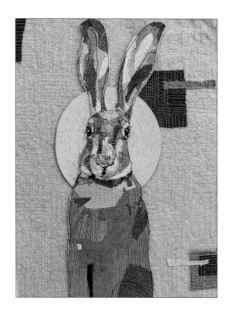

Cool background

The cool coloured background seems to recede, so projecting the hare forward. The pale blue-grey blanket also accentuates the warm colours in the hare's coat.

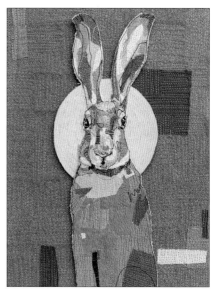

Complementary background

I think that this sharp olive green blanket background creates a vibrant, lively quality because of the subtle complementary pairing next to the rust coloured hare.

Arranging the background

The arrangement of the background pieces of fabric has a significant influence on the overall composition design. I really take my time when placing the square and rectangular fabric shapes before gluing them into position.

The fabric blocks in the example here divide the composition, creating visual interest, so helping to break the monotony of 'this is the background' and 'this is the hare'. The edges along the fabric block or stitching can also act as 'visual indicators' that can subtly direct the gaze towards the focal point.

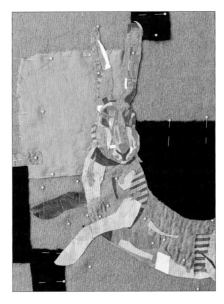

Avoid restricting the subject

You can see that the black strips of fabric really 'block in' the hare and detract from the sense of movement that I wanted to suggest in the composition.

Avoid tangents

If possible, try to avoid any background pieces of fabric 'skimming' any part of the subject, as with the fabric pieces that are touching the hare's cheek and ear above. Placement of pieces like this looks awkward, and detracts from the subject matter itself.

In the example below, the pink rectangle that appears to balance on the hare's back is very distracting, and seems to weigh down the leaping hare.

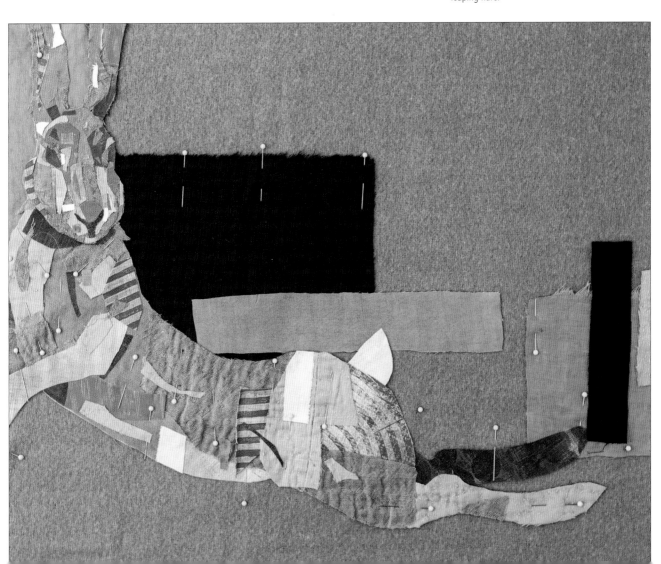

Composition of the fabric collage

Once you have chosen your colours and arranged the background, you can begin your embroidery. The notes below explain my thinking behind a few of the compositional choices I have made.

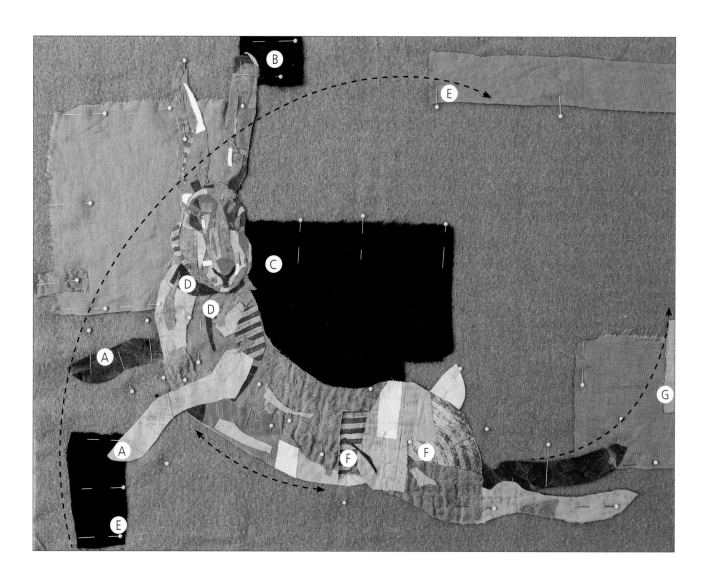

A. The more distant leg has been cut out from a darker fabric so that it seems to recede, while the closer leg projects towards the viewer due to the lighter tonal value of the fabric used.

B. The background horizontal black rectangle counterbalances the strong vertical direction of the ear, so creating a subtle visual tension, which makes the composition more exciting and dynamic.

C. The black rectangle placed behind the hare's back emphasizes the dynamic curve of the arch of the back.

D. The upward curve of the dark grey fabric acts as a visual indicator that directs the gaze to the face; while the dark shape under the jaw acts like a 'vignette' that frames this focal point.

E. The placement of these fabric blocks subtly counterbalances the upper curve of the hare, as indicated by the dashed line that leads from the lower left up and over the hare.

F. The striped fabric pieces help to suggest the muscular structure of the hare's anatomy.

G. The thin strip of pale pink fabric adds an extended upward 'flick' to the overall curve of the hare's body, so emphasizing the sense of movement.

Stitching

As well as securing the piece together, stitching adds to the composition. Allow gaps to create interesting shapes to shine through, and avoid being too precise when stitching straight lines. Slight variation helps to creates a sense of movement. Here, the integration of the background and the subject through stitching subtly unifies the two elements.

Scrips and Scraps Hare
68 x 53cm (26¾ x 21in)

A. Stitching the more distant foreleg as part of the background helps it to recede.

B. The scribbly black stitching adds a sense of movement and suggests a sketchy style of mark making that contrasts against the more ordered back-and-forth stitch surrounding it.

C. I repeated the curved line of stitching to emphasize the movement of the hare's foreleg.

D. The curved line of stitching here suggests the form of the underlying muscles. Try to not constrain your stitching by always keeping inside the blocks of fabric.

E. Stitching outside the edges of the hare in some areas helps to unify the background with the subject matter.

F. I wanted to sew the black outline along the hare's back slightly inside the edge so that the black stitching detail wouldn't be lost on the black fabric background patch.

G. Stitching in dark grey thread helps the back leg to recede. Using cream thread to stitch the underlying pink square creates a sense of contrast and drama.

Composing with sticky notes

A sketch can be used many times to create different poses and characters. I use my trusty sticky notes to create temporary additions to sketches, which can then be removed, swapped out or combined to try out various different possible compositions for my original sketch.

This simple technique allows you to build up a 'library' of designs and characters. It can become a valuable resource to help you to develop your work or to free you up if you feel creatively blocked.

Here, I used sticky notes to try out a variety of possible hat options on a lurcher sketch, giving me the ability to see how different costumes and details suggested different characters before committing to the final design.

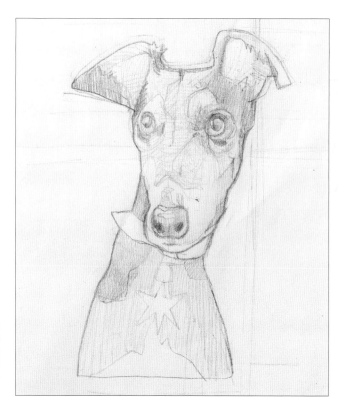

This is the original sketch, created very quickly on a piece of scrap paper. I didn't realize at the time that I would come to refer to this sketch on many occasions and create a number of different characters from it.

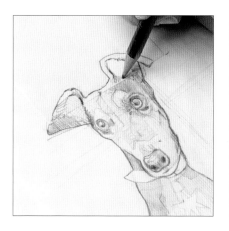
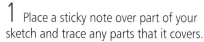

1 Place a sticky note over part of your sketch and trace any parts that it covers.

2 Develop the sketch further on the sticky note. Here I'm adding a party hat.

3 You can add additional sticky notes to develop other areas further.

4 The strengths of this technique are speed and ease of experimentation – you can easily take off the sticky note and try a different option.

Party Lurcher
10 x 15cm (4 x 6in)

I love lurchers and greyhounds; they move so gracefully
and they have such expressive faces. As soon as I started
sketching this character, I knew that it was party time!
This design was perfect for including a mismatched
selection of patterned fabric scraps.

Using sticky notes: Madame Pompadour

When I began using my sketch to develop a different character, I didn't realize just how differently it would turn out! Small changes can occur when trying out different ideas. Here the eyes seem much more demure and the addition of the body completely changes the overall feeling of the piece.

I thoroughly enjoyed creating the costume as this can be such an important element when communicating a story or a character's personality. I carefully selected and cut out the patterned fabric so that it would suggest the folds on the puffed sleeves. The trimmings and lace added texture and detail to her glamorous outfit.

The use of the sticky notes technique was key here; and you can see just how far you can take it in the image below, which shows a few different options which I considered for the hair/headpiece.

Madame Pompadour
35 x 60cm (13¾ x 23¾in)

Into abstraction

It can be really liberating to experiment with layering shapes, textures and colours to see what abstract designs begin to emerge. If an area becomes too chaotic, you can always apply a plainer, 'quieter' layer over the top.

Blackbirds and Winter Berries

I wanted to challenge myself with this composition and see if I could create a design that incorporated a wide variety of mark making and layers. I think that this design illustrates that, no matter how abstract the work might be, the inclusion of simple motifs can communicate a sense of place.

A. In some parts of the design many layers have been printed which builds up the surface texture and suggests a sense of depth.

B. There is a mixture of warm and cool colours, so that some areas of the abstract background recede and some project, which helps to suggest a fragmented landscape environment.

C. The polka dot pattern has been repeated throughout the composition to create a sense of unity and rhythm.

D. I printed some very flat, sharp squares and rectangles on the final layer in order to 'quieten down' some passages of the composition and to create some very strong verticals and horizontals which would introduce a sense of balance in this very busy background print.

E. The flat black printed areas have only been used for the two blackbirds and the dots on the 'hill' shape that the blackbird is standing on. This is so that the contrast in tonal value and texture helps to emphasize these motifs.

F. During the printing process some areas have been masked off and over-printed (such as this rectangle). This can help to create a sense of perspective, as though you are almost looking 'through' this area and into a space behind it.

Blackbirds and Winter Berries
43.5 x 35cm (17 x 13¾in)

Going further

The unfinished piece shown to the right is ready to be stitched – and it's here, at this stage of a project, that there is great potential to take your artwork further in a number of different ways.

   With the basics in hand, this part of the book explores how you can move on to incorporate more involved or unusual techniques and their subsequent combinations. I hope that you enjoy experimenting and playing!

This piece offers you a world of possibilities – how would you develop it? The templates on page 123 can be used as the basis to recreate this variation of the Patchwork Hare described on pages 66–69.

Paper collage

Paper collage is completely addictive and can lead to myriad further design possibilities. You can collage with vintage papers, drawings, photographs, magazine images and other ephemera you collect.

The technique itself is deceptively simple – you just cut out shapes from paper and collage them, exactly as for the fabric collage technique explained earlier. However, this belies the challenge: having so many possibilities can be overwhelming. My advice is to take plenty of time selecting and placing your collage pieces. This is probably the most important part of the process.

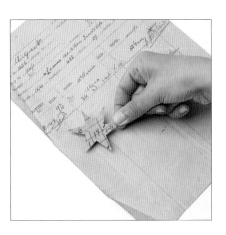

1 Test out arranging your selected pieces, and spend time trying out different options.

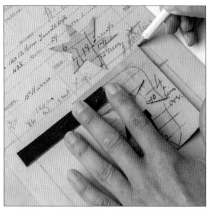

2 Use a pencil to draw underneath each piece so that you know exactly where it will go when you come to glue it in place.

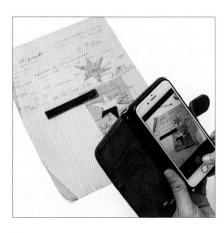

3 Once you have decided on the collage layout, take a photograph on your phone or digital camera before you remove any pieces. It's so annoying if you forget that perfect placement!

4 Remove the pieces, then use a glue stick to secure them in place one by one, working from the back forward. Try to apply the glue right to the edge of the paper (unless there is a lovely torn edge that you want to show off by leaving it loose).

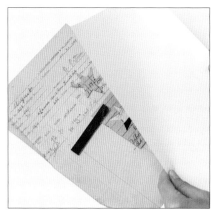

5 When you are pressing down a piece of paper that you have glued, place a clean piece of office paper over it first before you rub your hand over, this will stop your pencil drawing and collage becoming smudged or marked.

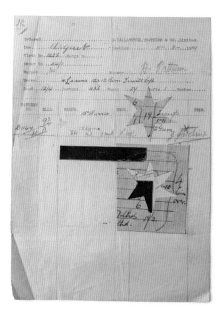

The finished paper collage.

Acrobat Mice

42 x 30cm (16½ x 11¾in)

This finished piece is a great example of how far you can take paper collage. Used alone, it is effective. Teamed with stitch – as shown overleaf – it takes on a life of its own.

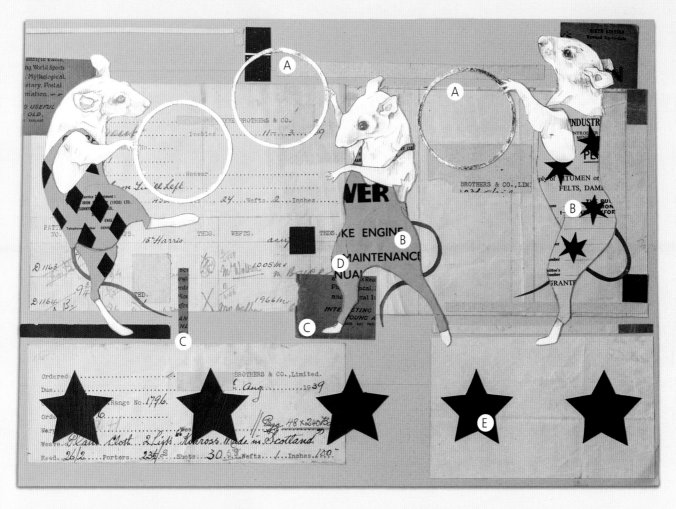

A. The gold hoops were made by cutting out the shapes in card, working over the surface with a glue stick, then coating them with gilding flakes. Make sure that you work on a large piece of paper because the flakes fly everywhere – and it also allows you to save excess flakes and put them back in the pot for next time.

B. I love to incorporate boldly printed papers in my collage, I think that the unitards of the mice really contrast against the more delicate quality of the pencil drawn heads and arms.

C. Try to use a particular colour more than once throughout your composition, if that's possible. This really helps to unify the composition and creates a cohesive colour palette.

D. I have tried to position the mice so that they are not contained within the confines of the background strip of brown paper; thereby their heads, feet and tails help to link the surrounding elements of the composition as a whole.

E. I cut the stars out of cartridge paper that had been painted in Mars black acrylic paint. This creates slightly textured, sharp graphic shapes.

Paper and stitch

A simple straight stitch can look very effective when incorporated into a paper collage. It can add another element of texture to the piece and you can create a wide range of marks just by altering the length and direction of the stitch.

Before stitching into paper, I like to pierce the holes first before sewing. This means that you will stitch in exactly the right place without fear of spoiling the surface of the paper.

Dib Dab Concertina Book
64 x 10cm (25¼ x 4in)

This concertina book is based on a picture I found in a magazine of a dab fish. I loved the quizzical expression and could imagine him muttering 'dib dab' to himself as he shuffled along the sea-bed!

I glued and sealed the picture onto a Moleskine concertina sketchbook using a matt finish Golden gel medium. When the medium dries, it creates a lovely transparent textured surface. I waited for the gel medium to dry before I stitched around the edge.

When piercing the paper with your needle, you can also decide whether you want the paper to be pierced outwards or inwards – this sounds very fussy but the punctures in the paper look more unified when they all face the same way.

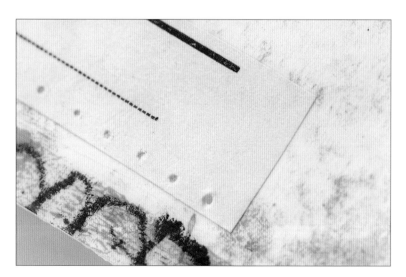

The piercings can be used as decorative elements in their own right, as here, or you can use thread to develop them into stitching detail.

Try to think about the length of the stitches. I elongated some of the stitches so that they wouldn't become too repetitive and I wanted to enhance the fish's quirky character.

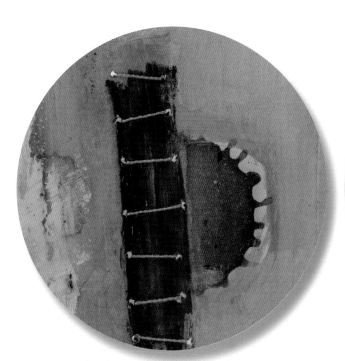

The pale grey thread creates a sense of contrast against the dark background. The ragged texture of the pierced paper's edges are also enhanced.

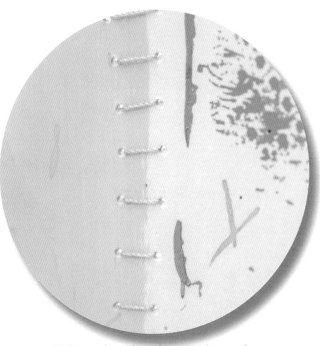

Stitching can be used to unify separate elements of a composition. Here it links the different areas and also creates a raised surface texture for added interest.

Gel-plate printing

You can create beautiful patterns by inscribing the painted gel printing plate's surface. This technique can be messy, so protect your work surface with a board. Before you begin, tape your fabric down to the board using masking tape – this helps to stop it lifting up and spoiling the print.

Lay out your acrylic paints in your palette ready to use. I'm using a stay-wet palette, but this isn't essential. The colours I'm using here are potter's pink and Mars black.

1 Peel away one of the backing pieces of the gel printing plate. I tend to leave the other one in place. It helps keep the printing surface rigid, and prevents paint getting on to the back – not a problem in itself, but it can get messy!

2 Use a large flat synthetic brush to apply the paint to the plate. Try to cover it thinly and evenly.

3 Dip a rag in your water, and use it to wipe off a shape.

4 Pick up the gel plate and place it face-down on the fabric.

5 Roll the roller over the back of the gel plate to apply pressure.

No roller?

If you haven't got a roller, you can simply press firmly on the back of the plate to transfer the paint.

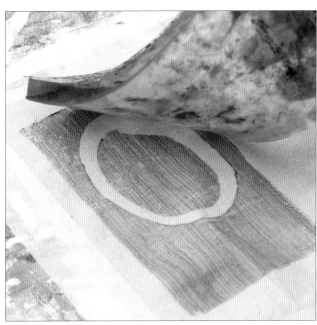

6 Peel away the plate to reveal the print.

7 Clean the gel plate by printing onto clean scrap paper until no paint remains on the surface.

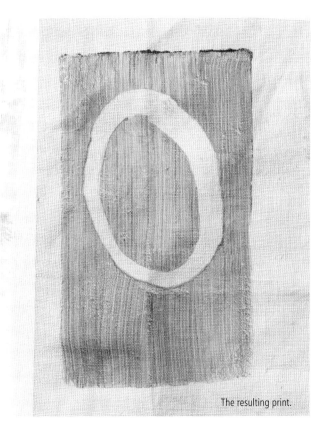

The resulting print.

Gel-plate printing ideas

You can experiment with a huge variety of tools and everyday materials, just as long as they don't damage or scratch the plate. One of my favourite pieces of equipment is the Catalyst silicone wedge tool. These are a great investment as they are so versatile: useful for both printing and painting.

Using a Catalyst silicone tool

Paint the surface of the plate as usual, then draw the Catalyst tool over it to remove stripes of paint as shown.

Gel-plate printing hints, tips and ideas to try

- When you first open up your gel plate, always keep the packaging so that it doesn't get damaged when you store it.

- The papers you produce from cleaning the plate during the printing process are really useful for collaging with later on, which is an added bonus!

- Whenever you are creating textures or patterns on your gel plate, experiment with whatever you can find (it becomes very addictive)! However never use any sharp objects: you don't want to permanently scratch your printing plate.

- When you are mixing your acrylic paint, try not to use much water. Your prints will become blurred and messy if your paint mix is too wet.

- You can use a paintbrush – a synthetic brush for acrylics is perfect for this – or a brayer. Try experimenting with both if you can, as they create slightly different surface textures.

- Once you have applied your paint, you can 'wipe out' whatever shapes you like with a damp rag. Again, an old t-shirt is the best material for this.

- If you want to create interesting textures, you can experiment by imprinting different materials, such as lace, bubble wrap, sequin-waste or hessian, onto the painted gel plate. You can also try laying some of the materials onto the fabric or paper and then printing on top (sequin waste and mesh are really effective for this printing technique).

- When you need to clean your gel plate at the end, squirt on a small amount of hand sanitiser and wipe over with a piece of rag (old t-shirt material is the best). Rinse your plate well with water and dry with another piece of old rag. Always store with the plastic backing sheets on both sides of the plate in the box.

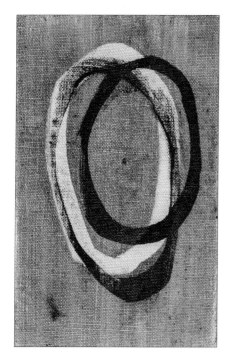

I used the gel plate to print two oval shapes over the top of the first layer, which was the wiped-out oval doughnut shape created on pages 54–55. Layering is a good way to build up interest.

For the first layer I used a Catalyst tool to wipe out a semi-circular pattern from a layer of potter's pink acrylic that I had painted onto the gel plate. I then repeated the process using Mars black paint.

I created this striped pattern using a similar process to the example immediately to the left, but I simply wiped out the lines using a damp rag.

This effect was created simply by wiping out the paint using a Catalyst tool in a wavy motion.

I initially printed a layer of potter's pink paint with the gel plate. Once dry, I painted a layer of Mars black onto the gel plate, then pressed the base of a cardboard tube (from a toilet roll) into the paint several times to create an overlapping pattern. I then printed this over the first layer of paint.

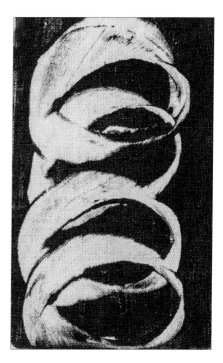

After I had applied a layer of Mars black acrylic paint to the gel plate, I placed the base of a cardboard tube onto the paint, before gently squeezing and twisting the tube to create an irregular oval shape. I repeated this several times and then printed the result onto the fabric.

Making a gel-plate printing sampler

Printing a sampler like the one below is a really useful way to record the techniques 'library' that you will develop when you start gel-plate printing.

A. Star stickers were stuck onto the plate, painted over and then peeled off before printing.

B. Star stickers were stuck onto the paper and printed over. The stickers were removed once the paint dried.

C. A direct print made from the gel plate, after printing over the stickers.

D. Elastic bands were laid onto the paper, then printed over with the painted gel plate.

E. A second elastic band imprint. This was taken directly from the gel plate.

F. Torn paper was removed from the printing-plate for this effect – this was the second imprint, which gave a fainter, more broken effect than the first.

G. A rag was used to wipe out this shape from the painted gel plate prior to printing with it.

H. Bubble wrap was pressed onto the painted printing-plate, before being removed and used to print with.

I. Printed masking tape was used here. I painted the design onto the gel plate, stuck a piece of masking tape onto a plastic file wallet and used it to print.

J. Mesh was pressed onto the painted printing-plate. The mesh was removed before printing with the plate.

K. Torn strips of paper were placed onto the painted printing-plate prior to use.

L. Cut-out paper stars were stuck onto the painted printing-plate prior to printing.

M. Here, corrugated card was imprinted onto the painted gel plate, removed, then the print made.

N. For this effect, I applied sequin waste onto the painted printing-plate, and left it there while I printed.

O. For this print, I removed the sequin waste, and made the second print directly from the gel plate.

P. Here, paper stars were removed from the printing-plate. This is the second imprint.

Q. The bird shape was wiped out from the painted gel plate, while the wing was scratched out with a pin once the image was on the paper. The legs were printed separately once the bird's body had dried.

R. The paint here was applied in the chosen design on the gel plate, left to dry, then 'pulled off' with sticky tape.

Using gel-plate printing alongside other techniques

Because there is always a touch of unpredictability to gel-plate printing, it is a really effective way to free up your mark-making – and to challenge any tendencies you may have towards perfectionism!

Cornish Herring on a Plate

This piece combines observational painting, print and stitch. The inspiration for this piece was a still life painting (see below) that I produced from primary sources. I wanted to see how this would be re-interpreted using these techniques.

For the embroidery, I cut out fish shapes from fabric and ironed them onto a piece of fusible web. I did not subsequently trim around the fish shapes, as that meant the fusible web acted as an anchor to stop the fabric pulling up as I printed onto the fabric. Remember to use your pressing cloth to protect your iron when bonding the fabrics.

To create the iridescent scales on the bodies of the fish, I used Daler-Rowney's interference medium (violet). Once the fish were gel-plate printed, they were trimmed and lightly fabric glued onto the serving cloth (the 'plate' had been printed directly onto the cloth beforehand). The gel-printed fabric is lovely to sew and the stitches really seem to stand out and pull the whole embroidery together.

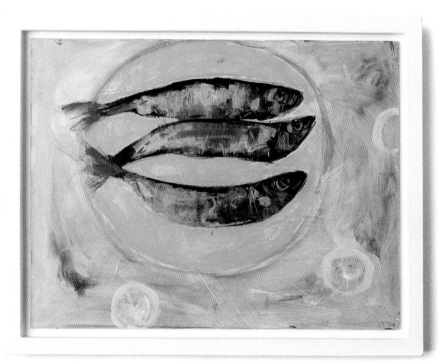

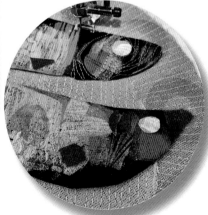

From painting to stitch

I enjoy trying to translate my paintings into machine embroideries and textile artwork. They seem to take on a different character and I enjoy the challenge of trying to re-create brush strokes into print or stitch. The images to the right show some details of the finished textile piece – compare the colours used in the painting with the textile artwork.

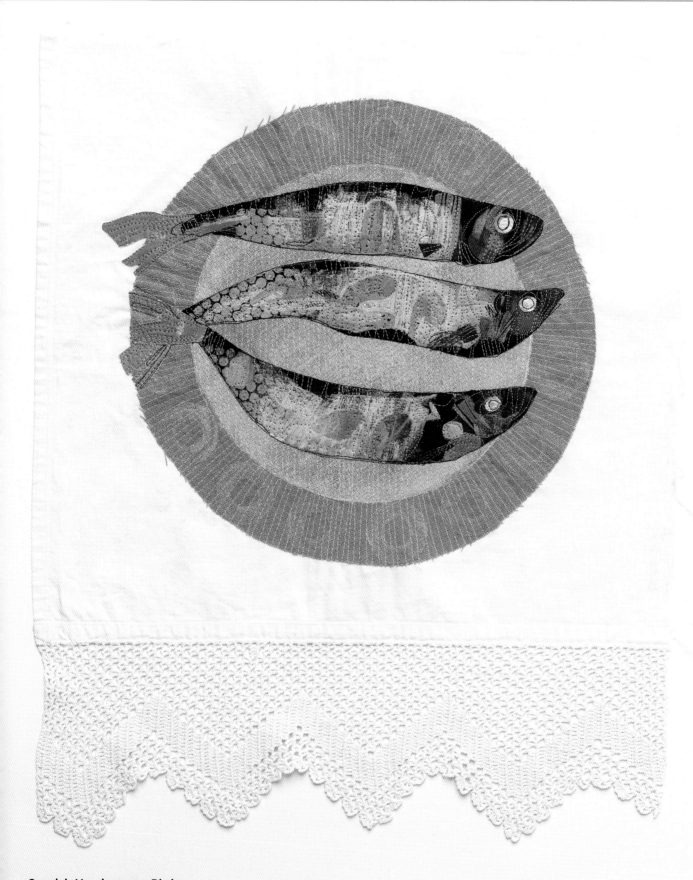

Cornish Herring on a Plate

37.5 x 45cm (14¾ x 17¾in)

I thoroughly enjoyed making this piece and it creates an interesting contrast between the painterly quality of the print and the linear, graphic quality of the stitched lines.

Making your own printing plates

It's very easy to make your own printing plates and you can quickly build up a library of different marks and patterns.

   Simply cut up scraps of mount board, apply extra-strength double-sided tape and stick on the chosen objects (elastic bands are my favourite, but you can just try out lots of different bits and bobs). Fine mesh materials such as lace can create delicate patterns, but after a while they can lose definition because the mesh gets clogged up with paint. Most of the printing plates are quite robust.

   Some of my favourite things to use on the printing plates are already backed with adhesive and so I don't even need the double-sided tape. These include those sticky foam shapes you find in the children's craft sections at the supermarket and, my favourite thing of all, corn plasters – I once bought so many the lady behind the till looked at me in a most pitying manner!

Ghost Hare

13.5 x 42cm (5¼ x 16½in)

Sometimes, the unprinted areas of the design are just as important as the printed ones.

By simply including a circular shape in the top right-hand corner and a series of horizontal stripes underneath, a semi-abstract landscape has been suggested.

Printing fabrics

You can use gel-plate printing to cover cotton fabric with acrylic paint. This is a quick and cheap way to create a whole spectrum of textures and patterns in whatever colour you need for a particular embroidery design. It also allows you to create the exact amount that you need, which is handy if, like me, you need to consider storage carefully.

For this example, I used a vintage cotton bedsheet as the fabric to print onto because the texture of vintage and recycled fabrics are perfect for printing and stitching. Of course, it is also much more environmentally friendly.

Because all of my work is intended as wall art, it will never need to be washed (as with wearables, for example), so I have used acrylic paint to print with.

Favourite colour mixes

The following acrylic paints were used for the mixes: Daler-Rowney System 3 titanium white and fluorescent red; Winsor & Newton Professional yellow ochre; Winsor & Newton Galeria pale olive; and Golden teal.

These were combined as follows.

1 Fluorescent red + yellow ochre + pale olive + titanium white

2 Teal + fluorescent red + yellow ochre + pale olive + titanium white

3 Pale olive + yellow ochre + titanium white

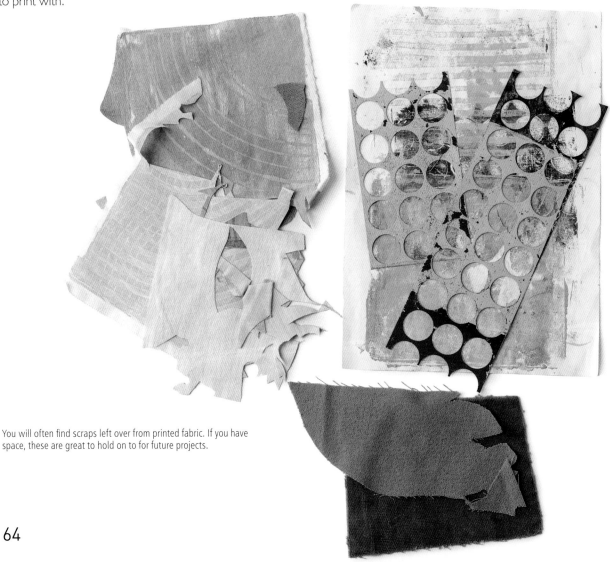

You will often find scraps left over from printed fabric. If you have space, these are great to hold on to for future projects.

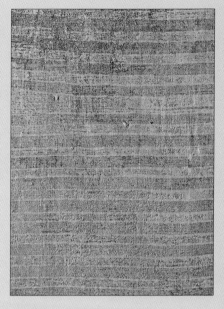
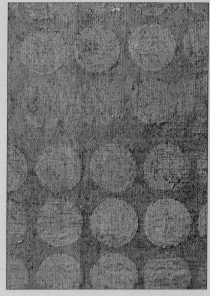

Making the printed fabrics

I used quite a limited colour palette when mixing the colours for the fabric blocks, and used the complementary colour pairing of the pale olive and fluorescent red to create a range of muted colours. This created a colour palette that works well together in an embroidery, as you can see overleaf.

I used the Catalyst tools to create the striped patterns and simply printed through a piece of sequin waste for the polka dot pattern. The layers of paint produced a textured surface, which is a highly effective surface on which to stitch.

Using the printed fabrics

I used the printed fabrics for the hare embroidery shown here. The templates are on page 123, and the techniques I use are described in the *Where to start* chapter, starting on page 14. I traced the head section of the template onto tracing paper, cut it out, and then used an air-erasable pen to draw around the template piece onto a cream-coloured piece of cotton fabric.

The templates are on page 123, and the techniques I use are described in the *Where to start* chapter, starting on page 14.

Avoiding sticky situations

Try to glue right to the edges of each piece to avoid it getting caught in the needle when you begin to sew – this can be very annoying indeed! Always leave the glue to dry fully before stitching.

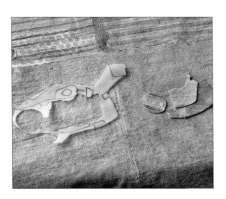

With the base section ready, I began cutting out one section of the head template at a time. I then cut out the pieces from the gel-plate printed fabric and selected the other fabrics.

I started with the head as it is the most detailed part – and an important focus for the piece.

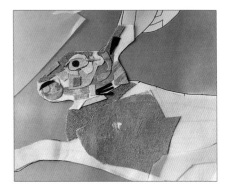

With the head complete, I built up the body on the base, starting by gluing the larger pieces on first. The picture below shows some of the compositional decisions I made.

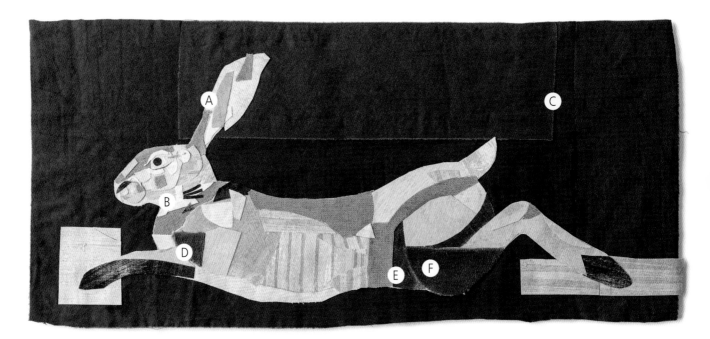

A. Choosing an 'unexpected' colour, such as the green printed fabric, can add a sense of energy to the design. It can be interesting to shake up your colour palette sometimes!

B. To suggest the whiskers I cut a small rectangular piece of black printed fabric and then cut lines into the fabric without quite reaching the other side, so that it could be splayed out and glued into place onto the jaw-line.

C. Once the hare was fully cut out and glued, I cut out the background fabric from an old dress and cut the same-sized piece from a vintage woollen blanket. I then lightly glued the blanket piece to the back of the grey fabric. I then carefully glued the hare onto the background fabric.

D. Don't feel restricted to using printed fabric on its own. I wanted the shoulder to stand out, as it would be a muscular part of the hare's anatomy, so I used a piece of mustard-coloured velvet to contrast with the flat surface of the gel-plate printed fabric.

E. I used the black printed fabric sparingly to help define the contours of the hare's body.

F. The back leg template section was traced and cut out using the base fabric. The velvet was used on the back leg to create a sense of three-dimensions again and to balance the shoulder area.

Initial stitching

It can be useful to draw a basic template if your design has several larger sections that need assembling. The reason for such a placement guide is that the design can look odd if the sections are even slightly out of place.

Before you begin the stitching, you can use the body reference templates to check that all the fabric pieces are in the correct place.

The diagrams also show the direction of the stitch lines for the hare.

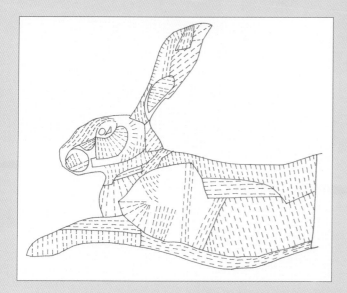

A. The patterned blocks help to add interest to the background and unify the composition.

B. Stitch the hare's face using cream thread. Try to suggest the structural planes of the face as you work.

C. I used a curved shaping stitch to help describe the contours of the shoulder.

D. Back-and-forth stitching in cream thread helps to define the leg against the similarly-coloured background.

E. The velvet really creates a beautiful surface texture when it is stitched: have fun and sew a dramatic pattern to make it really stand out.

Stitching eyes

This is when the animal starts to show its character! The pictures here show how I developed the eye for the hare, but the principles apply to almost any animal you wish to stitch.

1 Stitch a circle in the cream thread around the inside edge of the iris. This creates a little sparkle. Next, stitch around the edge of the eye in grey thread to create a little depth.

2 Outline the eye in black thread and add a small horizontal line to the inner and outer corner of the eye.

3 Stitch in the black pupil area. If your hare looks a bit surprised, it may be because the whites of the eye are too large. If this is the case, stitch a line of grey around the inside edge of the black outline, as shown here.

4 Stitch a small grey circle inside the pupil to reduce the starkness, then bring the eye to life by stitching a small white dot in the pupil.

Tips for eyes

The detail of the fox's eyes (above left) shows another example of the technique above in practise. You can invest a lot of character through the stitching.

As the thread builds up, you may find it becomes increasingly hard, even impossible, to work through. If something goes wrong, you always have the option of cutting out the entire section, as shown above right. You can then patch the work with a spare scrap of fabric and stitch a new eye completely fresh.

Completing the hare

To finish the hare, I carefully outlined the whole animal using black thread. I stitched over the separate body sections in cream thread, trying to suggest the form of the skeleton and muscles with shaping stitch (see page 24). I used zigzag stitch over the dark grey nostril shape – although note that I didn't use the machine's zigzag setting; I just controlled the stitch freehand.

The background was completed using back-and-forth stitch in a chequerboard pattern. Although it is all stitched in one colour, mid-grey, different block widths and directions create visual interest. Try to stitch in the background around the hare first: this helps to 'push out' the fabric and reduces the chance of the fabric wrinkling up.

Fading fast!

I used an air-erasable pen to sketch in the lines that I wanted to follow when stitching the moon (above left) – it is perfect to use in this way to help guide you around a curved shape. However, the pen seemed to disappear very quickly on the printed fabric. Fortunately, you can re-draw the lines during the sewing process as many times as you need (above right), so there's no need to panic.

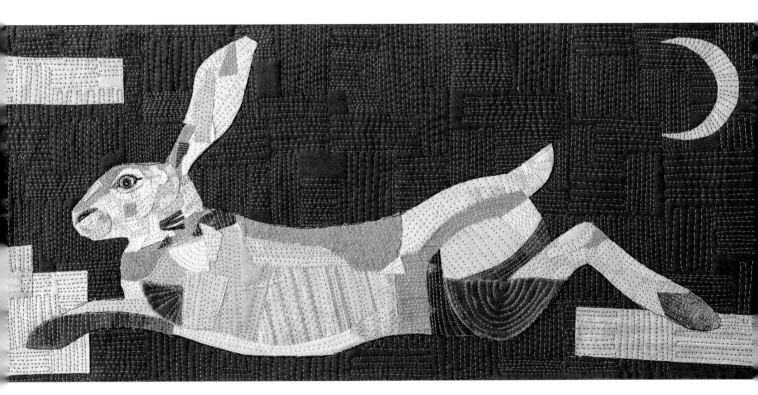

Patchwork Hare
60 x 27.5cm (23½ x 10¾in)
The completed embroidery.

Masks and stencils

Paper masks and stencils are such a quick and easy way to create more defined motifs in your work. A mask is a positive shape that protects a particular area. When you print or paint over it, the shape is left clean. A stencil is a negative shape that protects the area around a particular shape. When you print or paint over it, only the shape is coloured, not the surroundings.

I use office printer paper for my masks and stencils and I simply trace the design and use a scalpel to cut it out. Please be careful when doing this and always use a cutting mat. You can use the paper stencils and masks for a couple of prints but it quickly loses its sharpness. However, if you keep your original design, it doesn't take long to cut one out again.

Grey Running Hare
19 x 7cm (7½ x 2¾in)

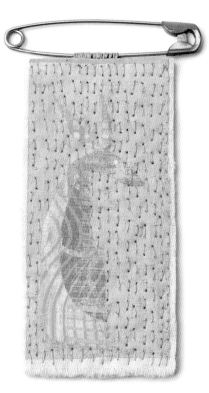

Mask and stencil hints, tips and ideas

- Over-complicated designs won't work well with this technique, so try to keep your shape bold and graphic.

- If you'd rather not draw your own design, you can trace around whatever animal shape or motif you wish (I have included a selection of templates that you can use on page 122). If it would work well as a silhouette, it will work well as a paper mask or stencil design.

- Before you print over it, use masking tape or sticky notes to protect any surrounding areas that may be accidentally printed onto.

- Apply enough paint to the gel plate so that the whole motif will be printed – there is nothing more annoying than having to print it again because you've missed off a tiny bit of the foot!

Hare brooch

I printed a patterned background and then laid the cut-out mask of the hare on top. Once the gel plate was covered in acrylic paint, I printed over the top and peeled off the paper mask to reveal the hare-shaped 'hole'. This can be a great way to use any left-over gel-printed fabric pieces.

Making and using paper masks and stencils

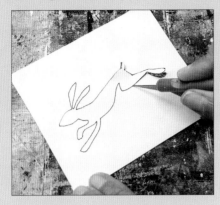

1 Draw out your animal shape and use a scalpel to cut it out. Remember to protect your work surface with a cutting mat.

2 This gives you both a mask (the rabbit itself) and a stencil (the rabbit-shaped hole).

3 Arrange the mask on your fabric. As described on pages 54–55, paint your gel plate and place it over the top, pressing it down with a roller before lifting it away.

4 Remove the mask. You can do this carefully, or wait until it dries to be perfectly safe.

5 When working with a small stencil, use masking tape to secure it. This also helps you to avoid accidentally printing over the edge.

6 Once printed, you can remove the masking tape and stencil at the same time.

The finished piece.

Positioning stencils

Positioning stencils seems simple, but there are lots of potential pitfalls, particularly on pre-decorated fabrics. I have identified a couple of common problems to the right. Spend some time arranging and composing any stencils before you begin printing.

This position is not ideal because the ears would be touching the horizon, creating an awkward tangent. Better to move it away and create a more effective placement.

Although this looks promising, I will need to move the stencil to the right to avoid the hare exiting the composition too rapidly!

1 Once you find a good potential place for the stencil, swap to the mask to check that the motif sits well in the composition.

2 While the mask is in place, place the stencil over the mask. This helps to ensure the stencil is placed correctly.

3 Tape the stencil in place to protect the surrounding areas, then lift away the mask.

4 Use a gel plate to print, as described on pages 54–55, then lift the plate away.

The finished piece.

5 Once dry, you can remove the tape at the same time as the stencil.

Positioning masks

When positioning a mask, bear in mind that only the space directly under it is protected. For this reason, you may wish to use masking tape to save any other parts of the printed fabric. I tend to place the mask, then use masking tape to create a simple box around the animal.

1 Place the mask and then box it in with masking tape, covering all the surface you want to keep clean of paint. Leave a small border around the mask itself; this will result in a clean, sharp 'frame' around the motif.

2 Use a gel plate to print, as described on pages 54–55, then lift the plate away. When removing the plate, don't worry if the mask lifts away – as long as you don't try to place it back down, your result won't be affected.

3 Remove the tape while the paint is still wet, as this will give you a few minutes to adjust the paint with a pin, if necessary – see 'fixing mistakes', below.

The finished piece.

Fixing mistakes

If the print goes wrong or bleeds, you can correct this with a pin by gently 'nudging' the paint into the right place. However, if the mistake is too large, you can lay the accompanying stencil over the top of the previously printed motif, mask off the areas you do not wish to print and then simply gel print over that.

Layering prints and combining techniques

When you first begin printing, the first layers can look pretty underwhelming. Don't be disheartened. It can, in fact, be a disadvantage if your initial layers are successful, because then you won't want to add more layers and push yourself. If possible, try not to give up on a print: it can often be that very final layer that saves the day.

The fox motif has been created by using a paper stencil. The background was printed using a combination of home-made printing plates, printing through sequin waste and using the Catalyst tools while masking off the areas I wanted to reserve with sticky notes.

Often the gel plate will form a fine layer of dried paint when you have been printing layer after layer. I love the texture that this creates, and you can see on this example that the surface is quite distressed and 'crusty' in some areas.

These are the printing plates, scrap materials and hand-cut stencils that I used to create this print.

Shadow Fox
17.5 x 25cm (7 x 10in)
Here I wanted to keep the palette muted, but I felt that some level of
contrast was needed, so I used a limited palette of warm and cool colours.

Reserving areas

One approach to printing that I find really helpful is to reserve areas that I'm pleased with as I go along. If you are printing on fabric you can use good old masking tape to cover up areas that you don't want to lose, or if you want to mask a more complex or rounded shape, low-tack masking film is great because you can draw the shape you want to reserve directly onto the film and then cut it out. I used this method for reserving areas on the *Blackbirds and Winter Berries* print on page 47. I always save the film once it has been printed over for future collages.

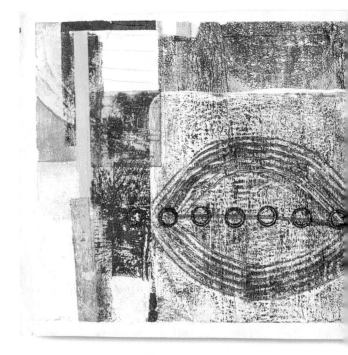

If you are printing onto paper I would advise you to use sticky notes to reserve areas instead of masking tape, as the latter can damage the paper's surface once it has been peeled off. I think that I use sticky notes in some form or other for nearly everything I do!

Applying masking tape down the sides of the paper before printing will help to create that lovely clean border when you finish, but always remember to peel the tape away from your print: you don't want to rip straight across all your hard work right at the end. Sadly, I speak from experience!

Whitby Kippers
53 x 14cm (21 x 5½in)

This piece was inspired by a visit to the famous kipper smokehouse in Whitby. The heavy-bodied Mars black acrylic paint suggests the tar-like walls of the smoke house and I simplified the shapes of the kippers by using a wooden clay tool to inscribe the painted gel-plate surface.

I used a strip of wallpaper lining paper to print on, I really love the texture and neutral colour of this paper and it is very cheap to buy a large roll.

I built up the layers of this abstract print and tried to incorporate the colours from the sea and the Yorkshire countryside.

Fabric hare sampler
29 x 26.5cm (11½ x 10½in)

I made this on a vintage piece of medium-weight cotton fabric and backed it with some woollen blanket so that I could stitch into it. I have used a simple running stitch in some of the areas, although I didn't stitch into the hares, as I wanted them to have a slightly three-dimensional quality.

You can see that I have printed shapes that I directly wiped out of the printing plate with a damp rag. I also used the Catalyst tools, printed directly onto the fabric using paint tube lids, and scratched into the wet paint with a pin to draw in the hares' eyes.

The hares and the stars were created using the paper stencil technique.

The small plant motifs were printed by wiping out the leaf shapes using a damp rag, and then printing the stems separately using the same method – you just have to be careful when matching up the stems to the leaves.

77

Creating texture

The two ideas here can be used to add texture in your embroidery designs. Both proved such useful techniques in my *Whitby Sheep* piece (see page 31) that I have been looking for new opportunities to use them ever since. While perfect for replicating wool and weathered surfaces, the effects could be incorporated into a wide variety of textile projects, including landscape or architectural designs.

Using Lutradur

A polyester-like fabric, Lutradur will buckle under heat. In the example below I have painted the piece beforehand, but this is not necessary. The paint may go through the Lutradur, so protect your work surface. Whenever using a craft heat tool, make sure you are working on a heatproof surface.

1 If you wish to pre-paint your Lutradur, apply a mix of Mars black, titanium white and Davy's grey acrylic paint to the top third. Add some more white acrylic to the paint mix and paint underneath the darker grey section, then use your finger to blend the edge and create a smoothly gradated transition.

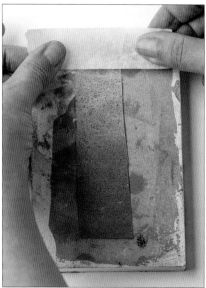

2 Secure the Lutradur to the surface (e.g. a piece of board) with masking tape.

3 Working in a well-ventilated room, use a craft heat tool to apply heat directly to the Lutradur – it will start to crinkle. Move the nozzle constantly over the Lutradur.

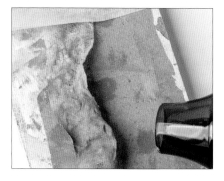

4 Reposition the tape so that the Lutradur is slightly arched if you want to increase the crinkled effect. Ensure it is cool to the touch before adjusting it.

The Lutradur is now ready to be used in the sheep embroidery.

Drilling

This technique works well with scraps of velvet. Work carefully, so that the drill doesn't snag or catch the fabric. I recommend starting with a slow speed to build up your confidence. Always work in a well-ventilated room when using this technique, as there will be a lot of dust! Before you begin, set up your craft drill according to the manufacturer's instructions, and always follow the instructions as you work. For the sake of safety, use a clamp to hold your work securely; follow the safety tips in your drill's manual, and wear any protective equipment it recommends.

1 With masking tape, securely attach the velvet fabric onto the scrap piece of wood. Use a clamp to secure the piece of wood, then get a good grip on the drill, holding it upright.

2 Working straight down into the velvet, use the drill at the slowest speed setting to bore a hole through the velvet. Apply gentle pressure as this gives the best control.

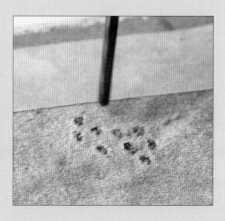

3 For dots, simply touch the drill tip to the fabric, lift away, then repeat. Remember to work straight up and down, not at an angle.

4 Continue building up the marks. Sometimes a larger hole will form but that just adds to the distressed texture.

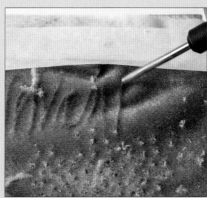

5 You can also hold the drill like a pen, to create a subtler surface texture. Simply swirl or scribble the drill (still set at the lowest speed setting), over the velvet's surface to create a two-tone pile.

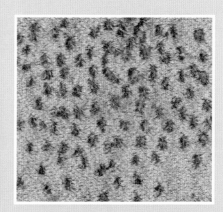

The velvet is now ready to be used in the sheep embroidery.

Telling a story

Stories connect us to our past, strengthen bonds and create a sense of community and attachment. My nanna and grandad were both from large families (they each had eleven siblings) and so there were always lots of family stories shared around the dinner table in my grandparents' kitchen. The tales would be told with great affection and humour whenever we gathered together, and as a result, stories have always been an important part of my artwork.

When it comes to writing stories, I never put pressure on myself – I soon found out that if I thought 'I must write a story today' then any ideas would disappear in a puff of smoke!

When I'm painting or sewing, I generally don't have a plan or carefully designed composition beforehand. (In fact when I start painting I never even know what's going to appear!) Even when it comes to sewing, the animal might change – a wolf can change very easily into a fox!

Sometimes it's not until I have painted or stitched the glint in their eye that I know who they are and what their story might be. If a story doesn't happen though, don't worry; they just want to keep their secret for a little while longer! Sometimes just getting to know their personality is enough.

Often what you leave out is as important as what you decide to include. Having a story, no matter how small, attached to a piece of work can add an extra layer of meaning to it. I think that people connect much more strongly to a piece of creative work through the power of narrative. Even if you don't publicly share the story behind the image, it can help to inspire further pieces – perhaps even a series of subsequent works. You may find that a story helps you to build up a collection of characters that pop up every now and then, all of which can be called upon if you are ever short of inspiration.

Starting points

I never start my designs with a story in mind, but remembering the animals' personalities as I am creating the piece will often prompt an idea. When I photographed the sausage dog and shire horse shown to the left, their characters instantly shone through. I initially sketched them to add to my library of sketches, without any immediate plans to develop them further.

Having such a library to refer to is an invaluable resource. Rough sketches of real animals will help you to explore your ideas, move things around, work out the most effective stitching directions and to 'push' the pose until you are happy with the design.

Vintage paper, old letters and documents are so beautiful and inspiring, and because the colours are usually muted they always seem to work well together. I love scouring car boot sales and charity shops but always look out for beautiful scraps of modern packaging, wrapping paper and magazine cuttings too. These snippets from everyday life can be fantastic for suggesting a story, investing a simple animal sketch into something with narrative and character.

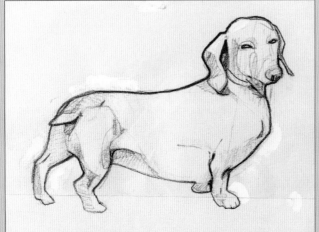

Sketches

Any of these sketches could be the seed of a textile artwork, and contain lots of options. The hare at the top, for example, could be cropped as a head and shoulders embroidery or as a larger, full-length composition design. I've really tried to grapple with the facial expression, to see what the character may be. Experiment with the direction of your pencil marks; this will be really useful when you begin to stitch. It doesn't matter that these sketches are so rough because you can move the limbs, exaggerate the pose and map out the background.

The Enchanted Forest

104 x 21cm (41 x 8¼in)

Concertina sketchbooks are so useful for creating abstract compositions, or for art that tells a narrative, because the pages can be folded in different ways to produce a variety of different compositions or designs.

The importance of play

Sometimes, when you need to generate ideas, the best thing to do is to play and see what starts to appear. I began this mixed-media concertina book without a plan, and from this *Enchanted Forest* concertina book I developed *Lonesome Bear* and *Ursula*, which can be seen on pages 102 and 103.

I began this piece by simply building up layers of acrylic paint and I continued until something began to emerge. I didn't refer to any reference sources for this piece, I just wanted to work loosely and mess around with my art materials! I remember feeling really 'stuck' for a while and I believe that the best way to power up your sense of creativity again is to get out your art supplies and play!

Here you can see how I have used blue acrylic paint to reveal the bear's silhouette.

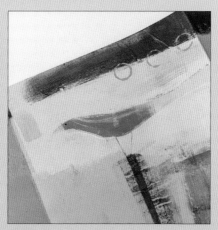

I have used the same technique here to create the bird motif. The peach-coloured paint creates a much more subtle effect.

There are many layers in this mixed-media painting and I have scratched through the top layer while it was still wet with a pin in order to reveal the underlying darker layer.

Stories, sketches and photographs

When you feel a bit stuck for ideas it can be very useful to look back over your old work, sketchbooks and photographs. For this embroidery I referred to some of my existing paintings and sketches.

For *Horse & Crow*, opposite, I scanned the pieces of work and composed a new design by combining the body of one horse drawing and the head that I drew for my collage *Lady Grey-Winter* (see page 90). I then added the outline of a crow that I had previously sketched to complete the design. The advantage of photocopying or scanning your artwork is that you can change the size to suit your needs and even flip the image, like I did for the horse's head.

The paintings above provided my initial inspiration; I chose to develop the horse on the right further. You might use the horse on the left as a starting point of your own, using the information on these pages – how would you develop her story?

Composing the design

I sometimes like to combine photographs to work from if I want a slightly different pose from the animal I've photographed. Some examples are shown below.

If you are able to take several photographs of your subject then you can simply tape the ones together to form the pose that you would like to draw or stitch.

Luckily this horse and raven weren't camera-shy and so I managed to take quite a few photographs of each of them!

The revised design

You can see here that I have simply placed the traced sketch of the crow and a cut-out scan of the horse's head drawing on top of the other horse drawing (pictured above) to create a brand new design.

Combining the two animals into one composition starts to suggest a narrative – and in turn, their character. You might choose to build on this and follow the thread, or leave it unresolved, to create a sense of mystery.

Horse and Crow

37.5 x 32cm (14¾ x 12½in)

When stitching in areas of the animals or backgrounds, I usually use the back-and-forth stitch (see page 24). Because you don't have to keep stopping and starting again on the sewing machine, this stitch can create a subtle patterned surface quite quickly. You can make the stitching as simple or intricate as you like — sometimes it can feel like you're stitching a maze! It helps to make sure that the corners of your fabric have been properly glued down, otherwise you'll stitch over parts of the fabric that have folded over which is very annoying.

Detail of the back-and-forth stitch. Note how it resembles ploughlines, tying back into the story to the left.

'There was once a horse who longed to plough the fields like his shire horse cousins. Every morning the horse would save a few of the farmer's seeds for his friend the crow. Crow would tell the horse all about his travels and adventures as he ate his breakfast, and then he would politely say his farewell. And because the crow would fly in such a straight line across the field, the horse would follow his shadow and plough the neatest furrows in the whole county.'

Acrobat Mice

Journalling experiences, memories or observations that you have made, writing stories or just jotting down a few descriptive words can help to spark your imagination and creativity. In turn, this can provide you with a path to develop an observation or idea further. These pages show the development of one of my works from a chance encounter on the street to a collection of artworks.

Origins

As well as sketchbooks I also keep a journal in my little studio – you can see it to the left, here. It was originally a vintage nature book and I use it to try out ideas, play around with materials and stick in those tiny scrips and scraps that don't seem to have a place to be stored.

This little character was quickly collaged into my journal after I had seen a street performer in Covent Garden, dressed as the Mad Hatter. He was sitting at his tea party, wearing the most amazing costume, and as he was about to take a sip of tea, a mouse popped out of the cup and ran around the saucer!

As we walked away after the performance, I became increasingly worried about the mouse. Was he well looked after? Was he tied to the cup somehow? I had to return and check that the mouse was okay, and after close inspection all seemed to be well!

I knew that I had to record what I had seen in Covent Garden, and this character has popped up in varying guises in quite a few of my designs.

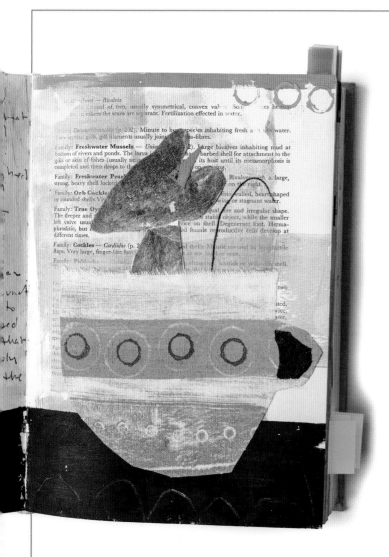

'The Mad Hatter's Mouse' journal page
For this collage I used a scrap of gel-plate printed fabric for the teacup and I constructed the mouse from a photograph that I found in an old book.

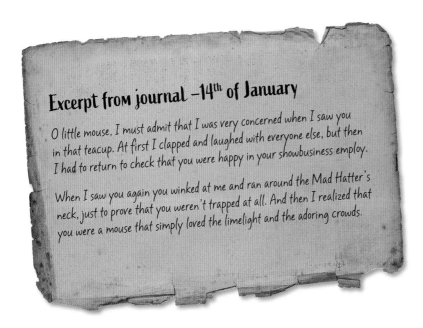

Excerpt from journal –14th of January

O little mouse, I must admit that I was very concerned when I saw you in that teacup. At first I clapped and laughed with everyone else, but then I had to return to check that you were happy in your showbusiness employ.

When I saw you again you winked at me and ran around the Mad Hatter's neck, just to prove that you weren't trapped at all. And then I realized that you were a mouse that simply loved the limelight and the adoring crowds.

Developing the idea

I find that it helps to develop a character by making your first quick sketches or doodles in different materials and using a variety of techniques.

You've probably gathered by now that I truly love sticky notes! When I am working on a piece, I often leave scribbled notes or sketches by the side of the work for when I'm able to re-visit it again. I find it useful to leave my unfinished work out on my desk, so that if a flash of inspiration strikes, I can quickly jot it down before it evaporates!

These very quick sketches of acrobatic mice were the initial ideas for the story and series of work and may well inspire further pieces in the future.

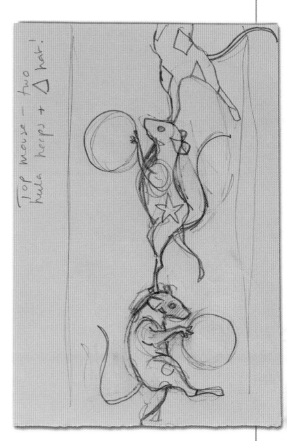

Early sketches

As I was sketching on the sticky note, little fragments of story ideas and possible material choices were popping into my head. It's important to jot these down as you sketch, even though those initial ideas may evolve and change.

Keep exploring

Even if you don't immediately use a piece, keep hold of your sketches. The sketch above inspired the *Mouse in a Spotty Teacup* embroidery on page 119. By sketching other possible development ideas on sticky notes I was also able to develop the sketch along a different line, which resulted in *Minuet*, the piece on page 118.

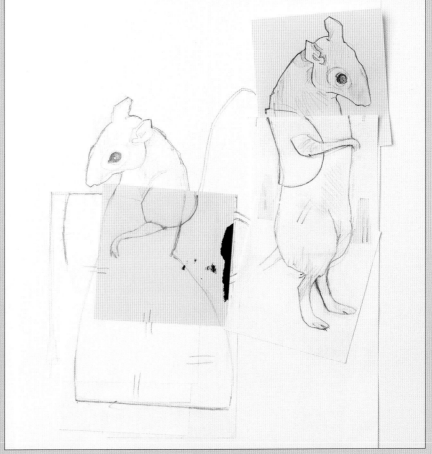

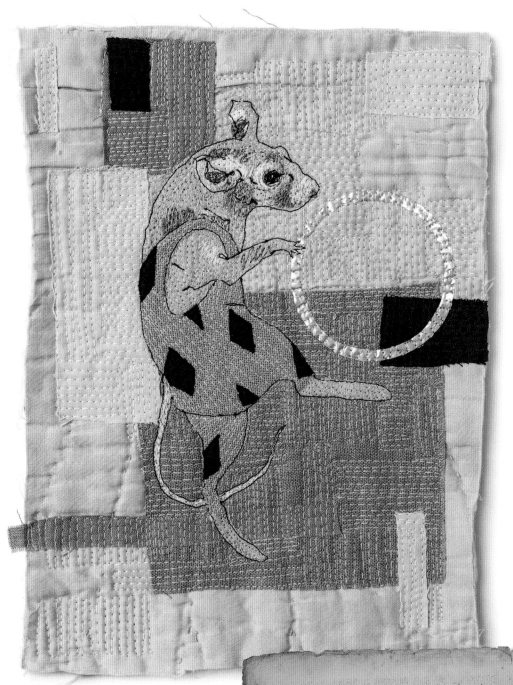

Acrobat Mouse 1
18 x 24.5cm (7 x 9¾in)

There once was a retired fortune-teller, Madame Luna, who missed the excitement and glamour of the travelling fair. Sitting in her cosy wooden caravan, as she wistfully looked through her treasured photograph album, two friendly mice decided to try and cheer her up. They hopped up on the table and politely asked if they could be of assistance. The fortune-teller considered their kind offer and a smile soon appeared on her face.

In only a few minutes the mice were dressed in fancy costumes made from one of her old scarves, and then Madame Luna opened her precious jewellery box. The mice gasped as they saw the glittering pile of gold and jewels and they were each handed a beautiful golden hoop earring. The fortune-teller let down her hair and swirled a multi-coloured shawl around her shoulders.

"Roll up! Roll up!" she cried. "Come and see the world-famous acrobatic mice!"

The two mice danced and whirled on the table top and performed the most skilful feats of daring and dexterity that you ever did see. And for many years after, Madame Luna and the acrobatic mice spent many magical happy evenings together.

Acrobat Mouse 2
21.5 x 23cm (8¼ x 9in)

Story and colour

I am frequently guided by the choice of materials, the colour and sometimes the text that can be found on the paper and ephemera that I collect. The materials that you are naturally drawn to can play a key role in setting the mood, character and colour palette. Try to be open to the direction that they may lead you, even if you have a strong initial idea in mind when you begin your piece. Don't try to control it too much because you never know where it may lead!

I love colours that are slightly 'mucky' and de-saturated; that's why vintage papers are perfect for my collages. However, your personal preference is individual to you. If you love bright primary colours, then celebrate this in your work!

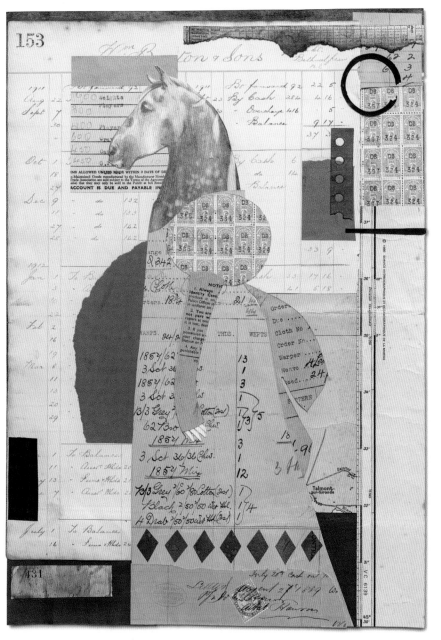

Lady Grey-Winter
29.5 x 41cm (11½ x 16in)

The elegant, flowing script and the warm, slightly faded quality of the papers I used for Lady Grey-Winter suggested a genteel, almost Jane Austen-type quality. I included some elements of cooler blue and grey-green paper in the composition to create visual interest.

To enhance the muted colour scheme, aspects of the compositon – such as the choice of a demure side profile – help to communicate the lady-like quality of the character.

Lady Rannoch
22 x 31.5cm (8¾ x 12½in)

When I started this collage I had no idea who my sausage dog drawing would turn out to be, but once I placed a coronet on her head she instantly became the formidable Lady Rannoch!

Red and black is a bolder colour palette than I would normally choose, but the post office book, vintage bingo card and old electrical instruction booklet suggested a regal, Scottish Clan inspired narrative. The use of the green background also helps to heighten the drama of this composition, as it is the complementary of the red elements in the design.

Story and style: old photographs

I have always been fascinated by old photographs, wondering who the subjects were and what happened to them. The costumes and formal poses also provide invaluable inspiration for character and composition designs.

Add a body and a costume and you have instant personality! The flattened, graphic costumes act as a perfect foil for the detailed, more three-dimensional faces.

The composition can become striking and dramatic by incorporating the simplified bold shapes of the sleeves, bodice and skirt or trousers. A side profile can look quite elegant and refined, and especially suits Victorian and Edwardian style costumes.

Composing Mrs Whipple

The symmetrical pose of Mrs Whipple suggests a more formal emotional quality. The balanced arrangement of the background shapes enforces this sense of formality. but the peeling edges of the paper help to suggest the slightly run-down quality of Mrs Whipple's boarding house. Take your time arranging your paper or fabric pieces, as the costume and background should work together seamlessly. Sometimes it can take me hours of shuffling before everything falls into place! It was the boarding house/hotel bill that I used for Mrs Whipple's bodice that inspired her story.

Mrs Whipple ran a boarding house for retired circus and music hall stars. She would listen intently to their stories as she served their breakfasts and she would sway from side to side as they sang their songs at supper time. Sometimes, when she swept the floor, she would find an old sequin glinting on the scullery tiles, and Mrs Whipple would become misty-eyed and sigh longingly to herself.

Mrs Whipple
29.5 x 42cm (11½ x 16½in)

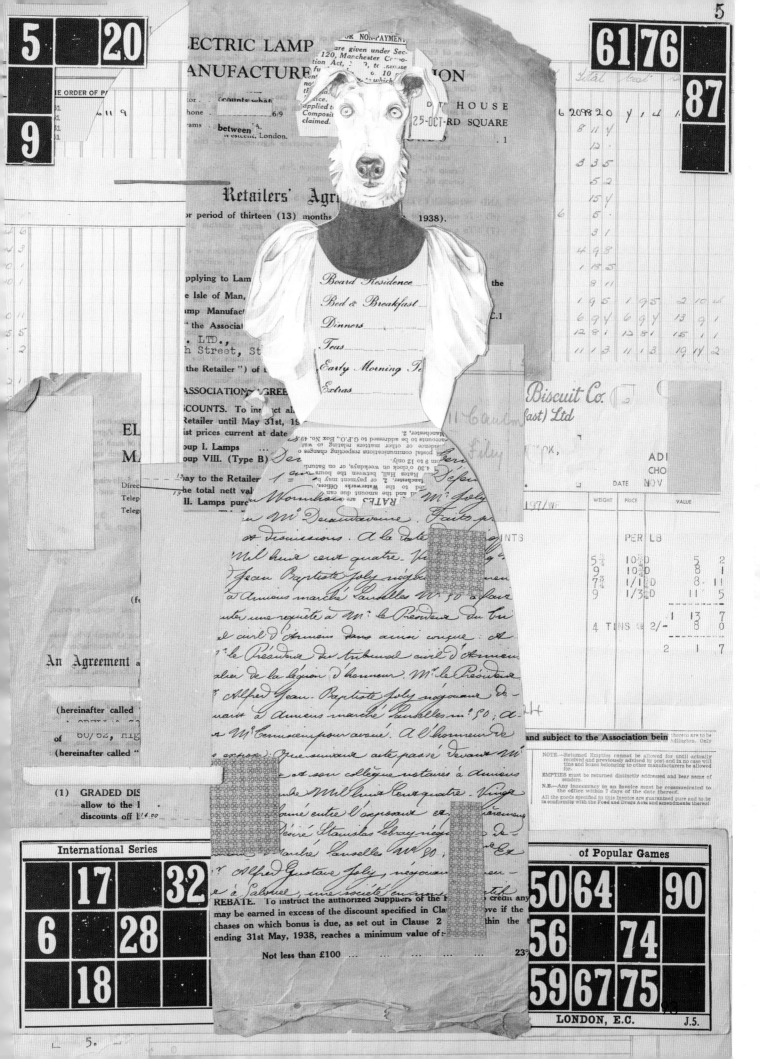

Sausage Dog

This project is an opportunity to combine hand and machine embroidery, and put the core techniques to work. This is a good project to start with as we use relatively few fabric pieces and add more throughout the process. This is a great way to build up a multi-layered, textured surface.

There are three main points to focus upon here: machine embroidering directly onto the base layer; the importance of the black outline for unifying the whole design; and not conforming to the rectangular format for the base layer.

The kilt pin I add at the end is optional. In addition to being a decorative design feature in itself, it is a useful way to hang up your work.

You will need

- Neutral coloured linen, 17 x 13cm (6¾ x 5in)
- Woollen blanket piece, 17 x 13cm (6¾ x 5in)
- Gütermann sew-all thread in cream, grey and black
- Gütermann Sulky Rayon 40 embroidery thread in dark grey
- Fabric scraps
- Air-erasable pen
- Tracing paper
- Embroidery tissue paper
- Sewing machine
- Fabric glue
- Scissors (for paper)
- Scissors (for fabric)
- Pins
- Kilt pin, embroidery thread in the colour of your choice, and rustic wool moire thread (optional)

My initial sketch
The template for this project, made from this sketch, can be found on page 122.

1 Cut out a piece of plain, neutral linen and woollen blanket – both large enough to contain the whole image – and glue them together with fabric glue. Add a small piece of grey bark-cloth roughly where the dog's head will be.

2 Trace the sausage dog template (see page 122) onto a piece of embroidery tracing paper and pin it onto the backing fabric.

3 Set up your machine for freestyle machine embroidery with grey thread and begin to sew around the traced template, starting at the head.

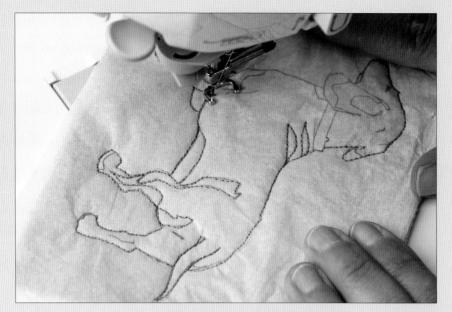

4 Continue working round the outline. Don't be tempted to 'fill in' any of the areas with stitching, as it will be almost impossible to remove all the paper afterwards – I speak from bitter experience!

5 Once you reach the beginning again, fill in the other small details. Whenever you need to begin stitching in a new position, it can save time to not cut the lower thread, and just move the fabric under the needle to start stitching again. You can then snip the loose thread afterwards.

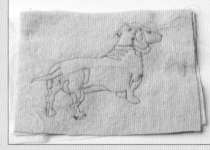

The back of the stitching, with loose threads cut.

6 Cut the thread and remove the pins, then carefully tear the embroidery tracing paper away.

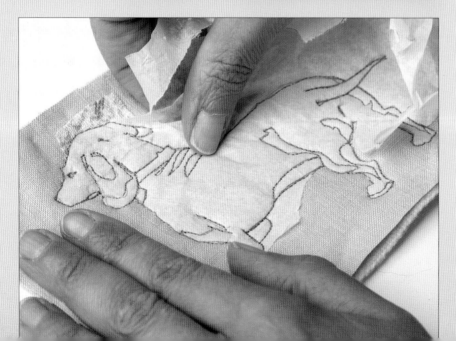

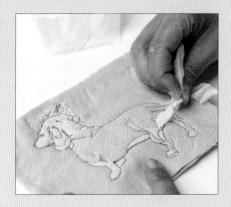

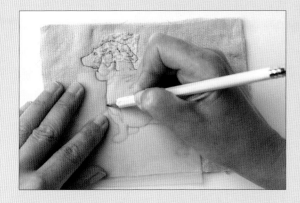

7 Remove any pieces of paper that remain inside the stitching.

8 Lay out your fabrics and cut some freehand squares and rectangles (or other simple shapes). Start playing around with colour and texture combinations and placements. Try to think about the balance of verticals and horizontals and keep moving pieces around until you feel happy with the composition of the first layer.

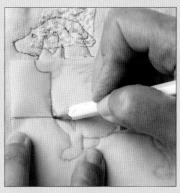

9 I decided to add a lighter-toned piece of fabric behind the left-hand side of the dog to help define the silhouette. To create these more precise shapes, lay a piece of tracing paper over the area, and trace the line of the body with a pencil.

10 Square off the shape to create a template piece.

11 Cut out the template piece.

12 Use the air-erasable pen to draw round the template piece on the fabric.

13 Cut out the piece, working inside the line.

14 Use fabric glue to secure it in place on the fabric.

15 Continue to add the small fabric pieces in the same way. I repeated the process to add blocks of colour, and cut into the dog's body here and there. It is up to you which areas you wish to cut into and define with the fabric. I added a darker-toned fabric near the nose to help strengthen the shape. You can also cover up parts of the outline, as with the pink piece here; we can re-establish the outline later. Thread up your machine with cream thread and start to use the back-and-forth stitch to secure the pieces.

16 Vary the stitch directions to add interest, and to suggest the form of the dog's body. You can create interest and variety by working some parts exclusively within an area (for example, one of the additional fabric blocks) and by working stitches that overlap different areas.

All the cream stitching is now in place. At this point, I have mainly used back-and-forth stitch to secure all the pieces in preparation for the next stage.

17 Thread up the machine with medium grey and use this to work the tip of the ear, using close rows of stitching that work right up to the edge to create a dense, filled-in area.

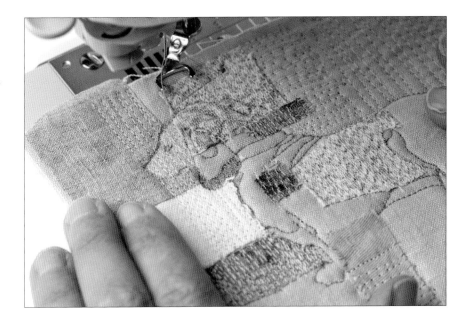

18 Make a new tracing of just the dog's outline on embroidery tissue paper. Pin it in place, then thread up your machine with black and re-work the outline. Aim to be accurate, but don't obsess about getting the outline precise – slight variations in the line will break up the outline ever so slightly, resulting in more personality and a sense of life.

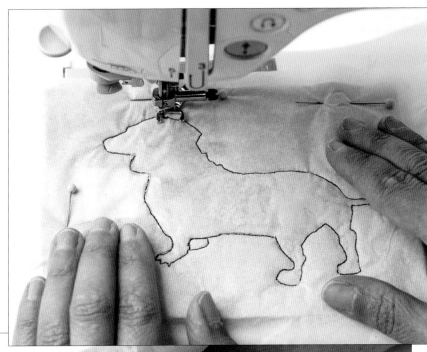

19 Remove the embroidery tissue paper.

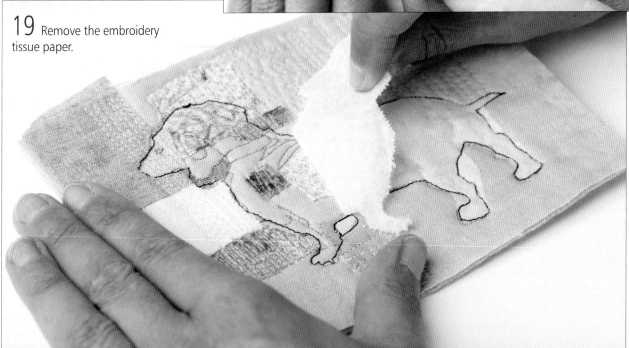

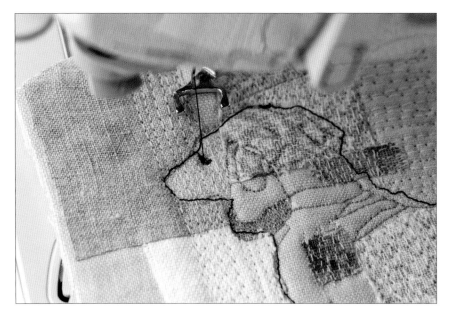

20 Fill in the eye with black stitching. Because it's so small, work carefully to preserve the shape of this important feature.

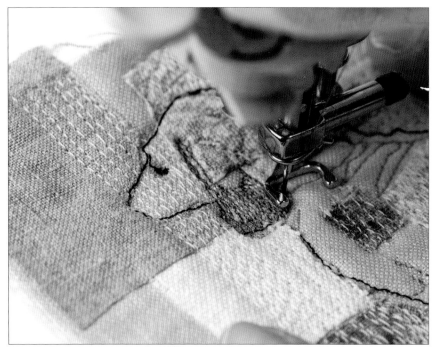

21 Thread up the machine with dark grey thread and stitch in details such as the mouth and lower half of the ear.

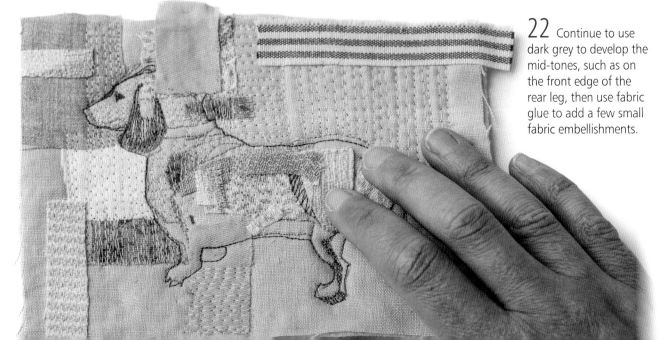

22 Continue to use dark grey to develop the mid-tones, such as on the front edge of the rear leg, then use fabric glue to add a few small fabric embellishments.

The finished piece

17 x 13cm (6¾ x 5in)

To finish, I added further embellishment by hand stitching with the rustic wool moire thread, but you can choose to include any extra hand stitching or not, as you wish. If you decide to include the kilt pin, attach it with embroidery thread using a simple blanket stitch.

Ursula

31.5 x 53cm (12½ x 21in)

When preparing to stitch Ursula's head, I used a similar approach as demonstrated in the sausage dog project on the preceding pages, placing the small scraps of fabric ready to be stitched, and continuing to add more throughout the process.

Lonesome Bear

28 x 40cm (11 x 15¾in)

In contrast to both the project and Ursula, there are very few layers of small fabric scraps used for the head here. Instead, a more 'sketchy' quality has been created that relies more on the descriptive properties of the black stitch outlines.

Midnight Fox

Building on the techniques practised on the sausage dog in the previous project, this project will demonstrate how to stabilize and embroider the subject before attaching it to the base layer. This will involve creating and assembling separate body parts, and also show you another method of softening tonal value transitions – this time with a lace overlay. The main techniques used are fabric collage, stabilizing fabric prior to assembly, and freestyle machine embroidery.

Save your offcuts

Small offcuts of vintage patterned fabrics can be a very economical source of a wide variety of colours – perfect for small projects.

You will need

- Woollen blanket, 38 x 35cm (15 x 13¾in)
- Off-white cotton, 15 x 15cm (6 x 6in)
- Grey cotton/linen, 21 x 24cm (8¼ x 9½in)
- Black cotton/linen, 15 x 19cm (6 x 7½in)
- Mustard cotton/linen, 21 x 35cm (8¼ x 13¾in)
- Yellow, duck-egg blue, pale grey, taupe, beige and peach cotton/linen fabric scraps
- Scrap of lace
- Tracing paper
- Tear-easy stabilizer
- Embroidery tissue paper
- Gütermann sew-all thread in cream, grey and black
- Air-erasable pen
- Sewing machine
- Fabric glue
- Scissors (for paper)
- Scissors (for fabric)
- Pins

1 Trace the first face layer template (see page 124) onto tracing paper, cut out the pieces one by one and construct the basic eyes, nose, ears and chin shapes from the cotton or linen scraps. Remember to use fabric glue sparingly. Cut the chin area of the mustard base slightly smaller, so that it is hidden behind the whiskers when they are overlaid.

2 Trace the second face layer template (see page 124) onto tracing paper and cut out the shapes one by one. Draw round each shape with an air-erasable pen, using the remaining template piece to act as a guide to where each piece should be placed. Work slowly and patiently; don't rush.

3 Carry on building up the layers on the face until all the pieces have been glued. At any stage of the project, please feel free to omit or add any other pieces to your embroidery.

4 The blanket is too thick for stitching fine details, so we need to keep the fabric layers as thin and few as possible. To help with this, build up a background from black and grey cotton/linen fabric, leaving gaps behind the fox's head and where the body will go.

5 Build up the body as for the head using the templates on pages 125 and 126.

6 Pin a piece of tear-easy stabilizer to the back of the whole piece. This can be torn away when the stitching is finished.

7 Thread up your machine with cream thread and stitch down the pieces, using the stitch diagram to the left. Try to suggest the three-dimensional quality of the head through the direction of your stitched lines.

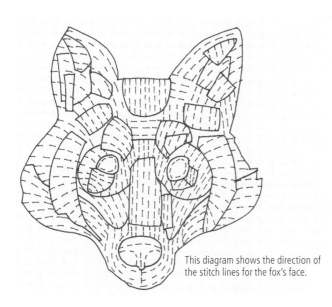

This diagram shows the direction of the stitch lines for the fox's face.

Contrast for impact

The black background fabric piece creates a really dramatic tonal contrast and therefore projects the fox's face forward.

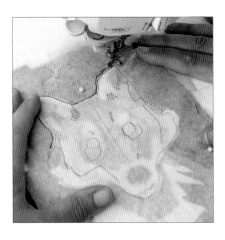

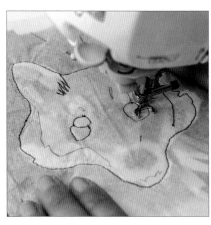

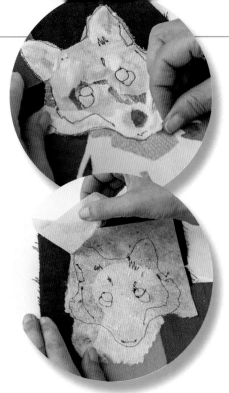

8 Trace the third head template (see page 124) onto embroidery tissue paper, and carefully pin the tissue paper over the fox's head. Thread up the machine with black thread and start to stitch the outline of the head.

9 Continue stitching the outline. Take the line slightly inside the edge to suggest a sense of movement – I felt this quirkiness suited the fox's personality. Once the outline is complete, add the main details from the template.

10 Once you have finished, trim the threads, remove the piece from the machine, and gently remove both the embroidery tissue paper from the front and the tear-easy stabilizer from the back.

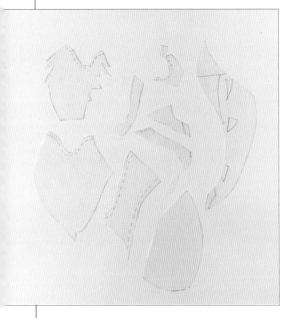

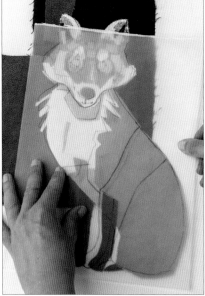

11 Cut out all of the body and tail template pieces (see pages 125–126) from tracing paper.

12 Use the pieces to cut out the fabric, then lay them on the fox piece, lightly gluing each in place. Transfer the body reference template to tracing paper and use it to help ensure the pieces are in the correct place – check before securing each piece with glue.

Body reference template

The reason for this placement guide is that the design can look odd if pieces are even slightly out of place. The template is provided at quarter of the actual size. You will need to enlarge it by 400 per cent on a scanner or photocopier for the correct size.

13 Start to refine the tonal values on the face using grey thread. Work slowly and carefully to avoid the needle breaking, and be reassured that the fabric should feel stiff owing to the build-up of layers and stitching.

14 Repeat the process with black thread. Continue to refine, building up the tonal range with grey and black threads. At this stage, the surface will start to feel built-up and solid, and it can feel quite 'jumpy' as you stitch.

15 Use fabric glue to secure the fox, the tail and the background pieces onto the blanket as shown.

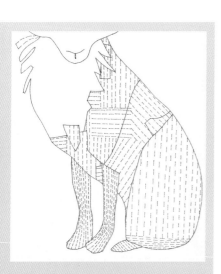

This diagram shows the direction of the stitch lines for the fox's body.

16 To finish, build up the stitching across the piece, using the stitch direction diagram. Use back-and-forth stitch on the background, and shaping stitch on the cheeks. To avoid taking too much focus from the fox's head, don't build up too much variety in tonal value on the body. The frayed edges and subtle stitching on the body will ensure it doesn't look completely flat.

The finished piece
35 x 37.5cm (13¾ x 14¾in)

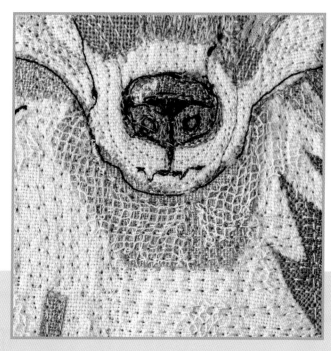

To soften the shadow under the chin, lace had been overlaid to create a dappled, textured effect.

I stitched grey thread around the eye to reduce starkness, and used white for the final highlight.

Even though the stitching on the legs is in thread of the same colour as the fabric, the texture of the fur is still fantly apparent.

The back reveals how thick the embroidered piece can end up, and why it would be impossible to stitch through too many layers – this is why it was important to minimize the amount of layers.

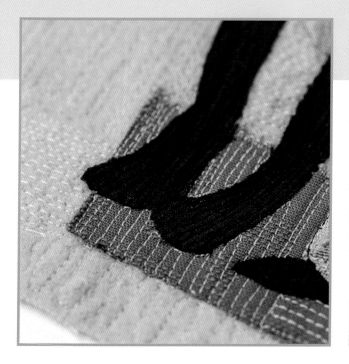

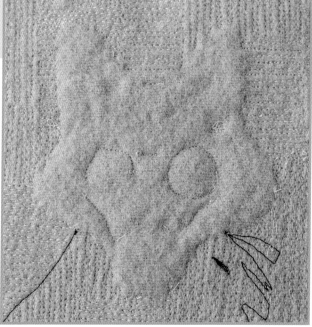

Cresent Moon Owl
6 x 12cm (2½ x 4¾in)
As an example of a different approach to *Midnight Fox*, this
small embroidery demonstrates how you can create very
intricate designs with very little underlying fabric.

Opposite:
Lady Foxborough
45 x 51cm (17¾ x 20in)
I used the same head design for this denim jacket
panel as I did in the project. By changing the body
and adding a costume, the design takes on a
completely different character.

Acrobat Mouse

It was a past student of mine, Charley, who introduced me to textile foils. As soon as I saw them, I knew they would be perfect for an embroidery based on my story of the gypsy fortune-teller and the acrobat mice! Finding new materials and techniques can be so inspiring and exploring their properties so that they will complement your way of working can be really rewarding. Due to the design's smaller scale and fine details you will need to use fusible web during some of the stages of the project, which will reduce the linen fabric's tendency to distort and move around when being stitched.

You will need

- Vintage quilt, 18 x 25cm (7 x 9¾in) (or equivalent)
- Taupe cotton/linen, 8 x 9cm (3 x 3½in)
- Mustard cotton/linen, 8 x 13cm (3 x 5in)
- Pale blue cotton/linen, 14 x 5cm (5½ x 2in)
- Green cotton/linen, 13 x 12cm (5 x 4¾in)
- Cream, black, white, dark pink and dark grey cotton/linen fabric scraps
- Gold textile foil
- Fusible web
- Tracing paper
- Embroidery tissue paper
- Gütermann sew-all thread in cream, grey and black
- Gütermann Sulky Rayon 40 embroidery thread (dark grey)
- Air-erasable pen
- Sewing machine
- Fabric glue
- Scissors (for paper)
- Scissors (for fabric)
- Pins

1 Trace the acrobat mouse template pieces (see page 127) using an HB pencil onto tracing paper.

2 Cut out the upper body tracing and transfer it onto taupe linen using the air-erasable pen.

3 Cut out the upper body and feet from the taupe linen, then use the fabric collage technique (see page 22) to build up the tones from white, cream and grey fabric (I'm using a mix of cotton and linen scraps).

4 Cut out from scraps of fabric both the unitard and the background pieces that will be placed behind the mouse.

You can compose your own background design, but if you want to copy mine exactly, the plan above will help you with the shapes and sizes of the background elements.

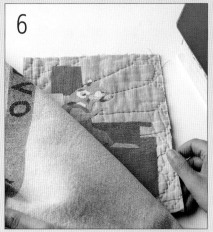

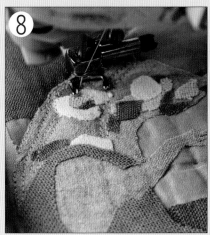

5 Following the manufacturer's instructions, use fusible web to secure the background shapes and mouse as one piece so that the design doesn't become distorted.

6 Check if any excess fusible web needs trimming, then bond the piece to the base layer.

7 Add any additional fabric elements to the mouse and background, securing them with fabric glue. Here I'm adding a little black patch on the pink square above the mouse, and a pink patch on the mouse's cheek.

8 Set up your sewing machine for freestyle machine embroidery (see page 24) with cream thread in both the top and the bottom bobbin. Begin to stitch the mouse's face with shaping stitch (see page 24) to suggest the form.

9 Once you've stitched the head, move on to the next area. Try to follow the flow, stitching down one area before moving on to the next. Here, the needle ended up near a section of background, so I starting working a section of back-and-forth stitch.

10 Use dark grey thread to develop the darker tones on the head. Refer to the diagram to the right to help with your choice of stitch, and use the stitch direction to suggest the planes and angles of the face.

This diagram shows the direction of the stitch lines.

11 Change to light grey thread and knock back the starkness of the dark grey thread on the head, working until this important focal area is complete.

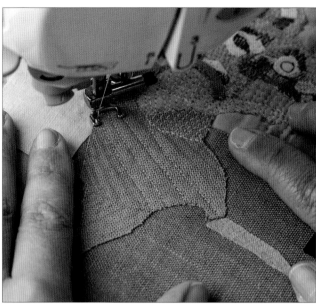

12 Change to a cream thread for the leotard, working long straight lines down the leg. You may find it handy to draw guide lines on first, using an air-erasable pen.

13 Build up the stitching across the rest of the picture in the same way, then use fusible web to attach small black fabric diamonds to the mouse's unitard. Once secure, use black thread to stitch around them, not over them, to ensure they don't become distorted.

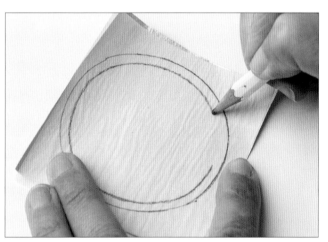

14 Secure a piece of fusible web to the back of a piece of textile foil, then use a pencil to draw circles on the backing a little way in from the edge.

Drawing circles

I found it useful to draw around a jar lid for the outer circle, and then hand draw the inner circle.

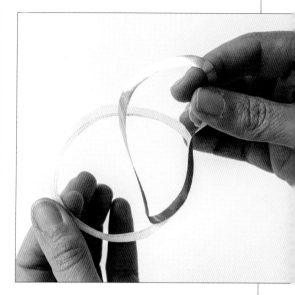

15 Fold the bonded foil in half and cut into the central hole as shown.

16 Unfold the foil and cut outwards from the centre to the inner circle.

17 Cut all the way round to remove the centre, then cut around the outer edge. Next, remove the remaining backing.

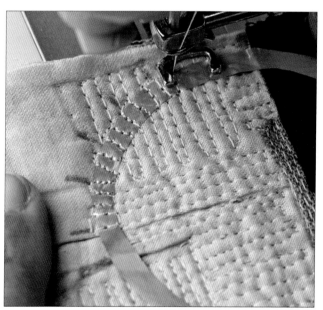

18 Use the iron to secure the fusible web hoop in place over the mouse's hand, then use an air-erasable pen to make marks like a clockface around the hoop. These wll help you to create evenly-angled stitches around the hoop.

19 Use the guides to stitch over the hoop, using cream thread. The foil is quite delicate; if you simply machine stitched over the top in a circle, the foil would be crushed. To avoid this, work back-and-forth stitching over the hoop, using the vertical stitches to trap the hoop.

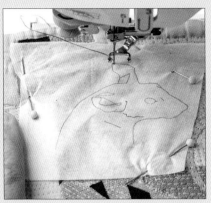

20 Change to black thread on the machine and outline the arm, working freehand. When you come to the hand, carefully stitch the fingers so that they overlap the gold hoop.

21 Trace the head onto embroidery tissue paper and pin it in place.

22 Outline the head carefully. Don't work the stitch too densely, or you'll have trouble removing the paper.

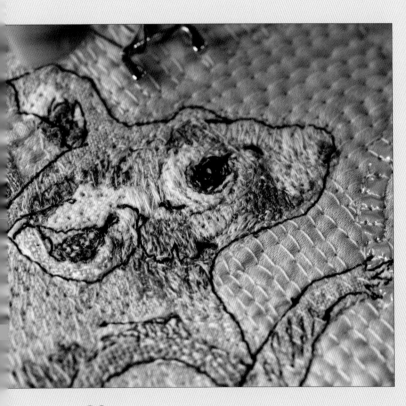

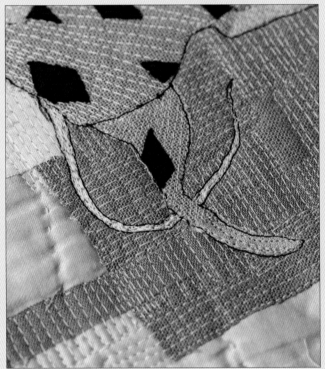

23 Once you have removed the paper, work the eye by filling it in very densely. Towards the edge of the pupil, make the stitching sparser, so you get a sense of light.

24 Use black thread to outline the rest of the body and stitch the tail freehand, then fill it with grey and cream thread to finish.

Tip

If you accidentally over-work the eye and make it too dark and dense, you can work in a lighter thread as a highlight.

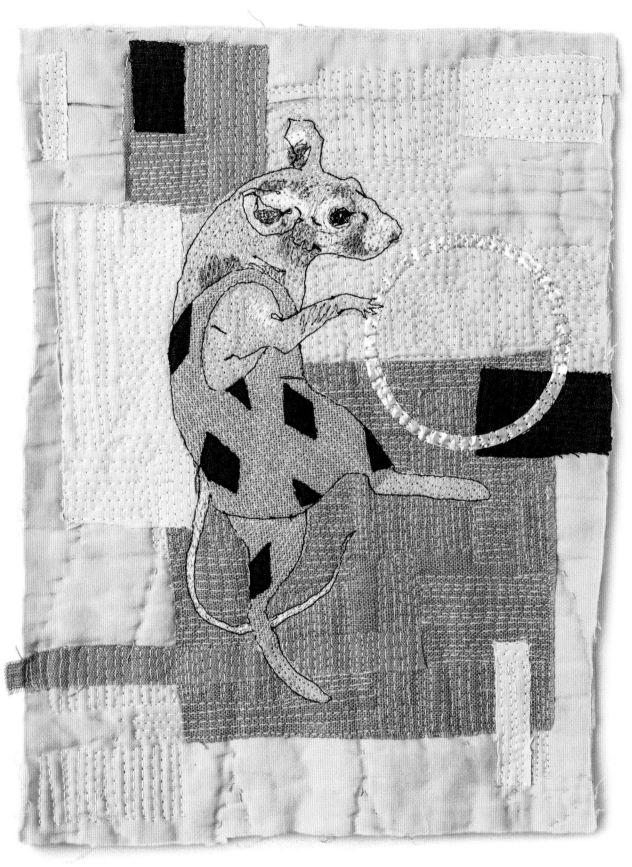

The finished piece
19 x 24.5cm (7½ x 9¾in)

Minuet

26 x 29cm (10¼ x 11½in)

I have used the same techniques as the project to create this embroidery – but you can see how
the overall feel of the design is completely changed by using a different colour palette.

Mouse in a Spotty Teacup
16.5 x 20cm (6½ x 8in)

I enjoyed the juxtaposition of the detailed, layered stitching on the mouse's face set next to the flat, simplified teacup shape. I gel-plate printed the green spots on the cup – I like how the underlying pattern of the fabric just shows through.

Afterword

One of my life-long dreams has been to write a book, and it has been a real privilege to share my inspiration, stories and processes with you. I hope that you have enjoyed experimenting with the techniques that have been covered, and that you will go on to use them and make them your own.

I hope that this book inspires you to see all the possibilities that are open to you when you create using stitch, print or collage and that you can share your unique stories, whether they are written down in words or silently woven into your creations.

Presenting your work

Whenever I am in a charity shop, or trawling through a car boot sale, I always keep my eye open for things that I could use to hang or display my work. Old wooden coat hangers, kilt pins and clips provide interesting ways to hang up your textile art.

I was also really pleased to find this large vintage purse, which was just the right size to pin on the 'Party Lurcher' embroidery, because the clasp is perfect for hanging on a nail!

Varvinter
20.5 x 29cm (8¼ x 11½in)

Pencil drawn head. Vintage paper collage. This is the collage that inspired the Varvinter embroidery on page 27. This portrayal of the same character evokes a different emotional quality, owing to the use of a different technique, colour palette and costume design. I feel as though she is a strong matriarch here, instead of the more demure maiden that emerged in the embroidery version.

Here, the arms have a 'negative cut-out' quality because I've used the same type of paper that was used for the background. The overall composition is quite symmetrical, but because I don't like to use a ruler it seems slightly 'off' which is an effect that I prefer in my designs. The torn edges seem to counterbalance the very sharp, straight edges throughout the piece. I've embellished the bodice and sleeves of her costume using scraps of an old plastic doily (one of my favourite ever materials to collage with)!

Templates

All templates are provided at full size, except where noted.

Small animal templates

These small animal templates are ideal for using to create masks or stencils for gel-plate printing. They are used within or as focal points in the following pieces, if you want further inspiration: *Ghost Hare* on page 63; *Grey Running Hare* and *Hare Brooch* on page 70; *Shadow Fox* on page 75; and the fabric hare sampler on page 76.

Sausage Dog template

This template is used for the project on pages 94–101.

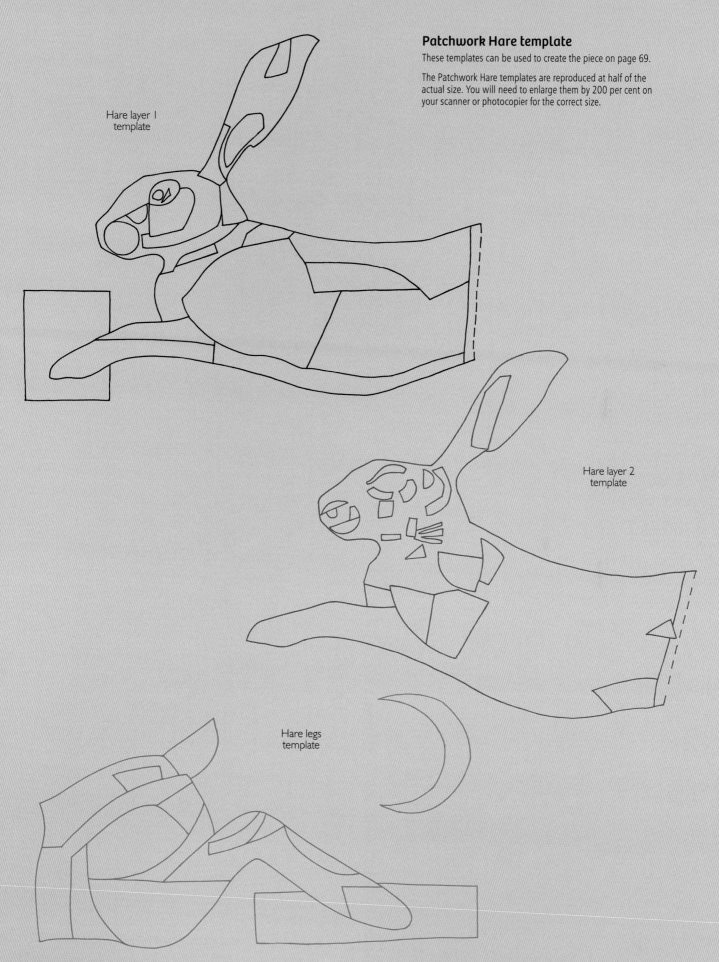

Hare layer 1 template

Patchwork Hare template
These templates can be used to create the piece on page 69.

The Patchwork Hare templates are reproduced at half of the actual size. You will need to enlarge them by 200 per cent on your scanner or photocopier for the correct size.

Hare layer 2 template

Hare legs template

123

Face layer 1 template

Midnight Fox templates
These templates are used for the project on pages 104–109.

Face layer 3 template

Face layer 2 template

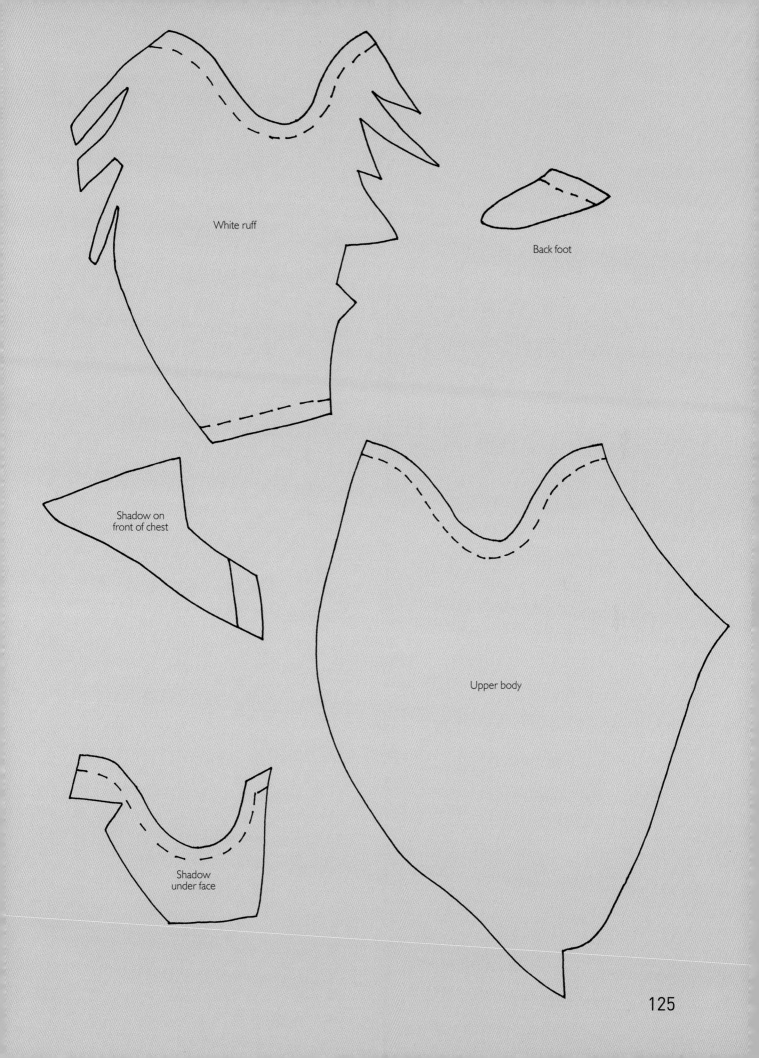

White ruff

Back foot

Shadow on
front of chest

Upper body

Shadow
under face

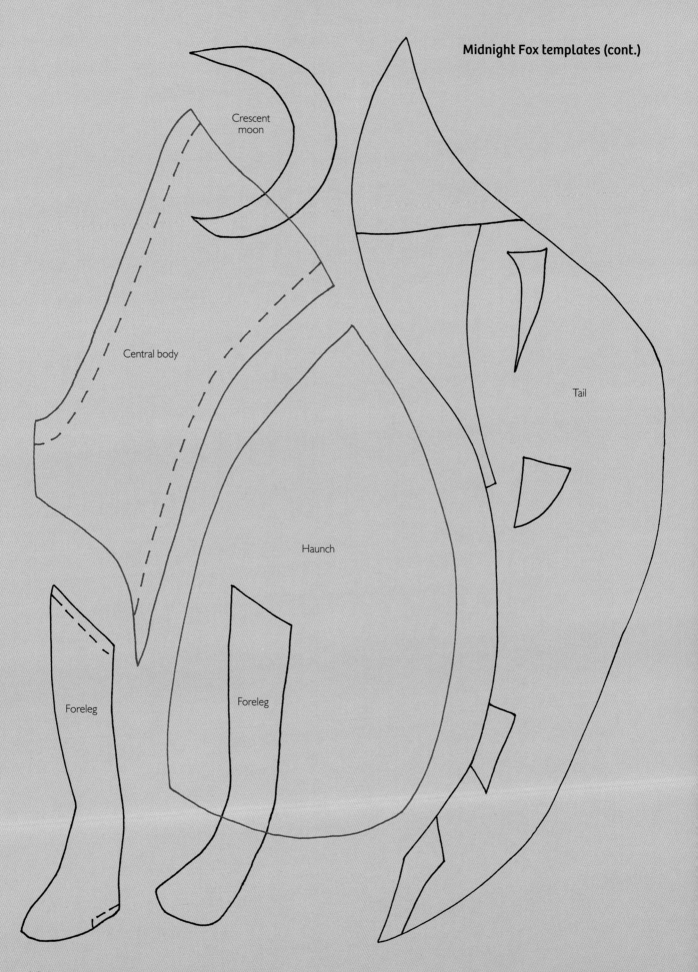

Crescent
moon

Central body

Haunch

Tail

Foreleg

Foreleg

Acrobat Mouse templates

These templates are used for the project on pages 112–117.

Index